GW00871155

How to
a Non-Fiction Kindle
eBook in 15 Days

Your Step-by-Step Guide to Writing
a Non-Fiction eBook that Sells!

Akash P. Karia

#1 Internationally Bestselling Author of

"Anti-Procrastination for Writers" and

"How to Effortlessly Write 1000+ Words - Per HOUR"

www.AkashKaria.com

Bestselling Books by Akash Karia

Available on Amazon (www.bit.ly/AkashKaria):

Anti-Procrastination for Writers

How to Effortlessly Write 1000+ Words - Per HOUR: The 1K+ Writing System for Writing Nonfiction Books Faster!

How to Deliver a Great TED Talk

How to Design TED-Worthy Presentation Slides

Own the Room: Presentation Techniques to Keep Your Audience on the Edge of Their Seats

How Successful People Think Differently

ANTI Negativity: How to Stop Negative Thinking and Lead a Positive Life

Persuasion Psychology: 26 Powerful Techniques to Persuade Anyone!

The Fine Art of Small Talk

FREE RESOURCES

There are hundreds of free articles as well as several eBooks, MP3s and videos on Akash's blog. To get instant access to those, head over to www.AkashKaria.com.

RAVE REVIEW FROM READERS FOR "HOW TO WRITE A NON-FICTION KINDLE EBOOK IN 15 DAYS"

"I tried to write a non-fiction book once. It didn't sell. Within 15 minutes of reading this book I realized why. This book won't write your book for you... but it will help you get the book done, and you will sell more copies. Buying this book is a no-brainer. For the price of the book - you will need to sell somewhere between 1 and 5 more books to recoup the investment. You'll sell way more than that."
~ Phil Barth

"Akash has nailed down 82 straight-forward steps to complete in 15 days to create a non-fiction book. **As an author writing as from experience, his steps are proven and easy to follow**. I particularly like that he offers bonus day-16, which helps with the publishing task."
~ Donna Hook

"Reading this book gave me [new] ideas as I am about to publish the eBook version of my newest book, 'Business, Brains & BS'. **I immediately made some changes based on Akash 's book.**"
~ Hazel Wagner

"**Great book**. This book is helping me immensely."
~ John Harry Thomas

"The book is well structured, and offers excellent tips on not only how to write your book, but also how to promote it (which is the tough part!). It's a lot of work, but it's clear that Akash takes the experience seriously and has success to show for it. **Definitely recommended to anyone hoping to write an eBook. I can't wait to get started on mine!"**
~ Margaret La

"I am using this book to write my second ebook (my first one sold, but not as well as I'd like)...this is going to be just what I needed. **I'm already learning techniques I never knew about. Excellent resource..."**
~ Paul Cola

"I love this book! Akash shows you a step by step [approach] on how to write a great Kindle book."
~ Jonathan Li, bestselling author of Secrets of the Confident Speaker

CONTENTS

YOUR FREE GIFT

As a way of saying thank you for your purchase, I'd like to offer you a free bonus package worth $297. This bonus package contains eBooks, videos and audiotapes on how to overcome procrastination and triple your productivity. You can download the free bonus here:

www.AkashKaria.com/FREE

For Mum and Dad,
Paresh and Nisha Karia.
I remember when
At the age of 14,
I wrote my first short story and told you
I was going to submit it to Penguin for publishing.
Instead of laughing at me,
And discarding a fourteen year-old's starry ambitions,
You paid for the postage
And told me how proud you were.

Penguin never published that book,
But here we are
Fourteen published books later,
And a dream-career that came true
Because you told me that there was
No reason it couldn't.

Chapter One

HAVE YOU SECRETLY WANTED TO WRITE A BESTSELLING BOOK?

Have you always secretly wanted to write a best-selling book? Do you feel a rush of excitement when you think about making money from your words on the page? If so, you're just 15 days away from being able to make this dream into a reality.

The prospect of creating and publishing your own book may be a bit overwhelming. But by following the simple steps outlined below, you will bite off one piece of your project at a time – until you are a published author!

In this step-by-step, day-by-day guide, you will discover how to:

- Pick the best niche to maximize your sales

- **Quickly assess the demand and profitability of your book**

- Say goodbye to writer's block once and for all

- **Research your topic like a pro using four great online tools**

- Easily and painlessly outline your book

- **Craft powerful book titles that generate sales**

- Use Facebook, Twitter and A/B testing to discover the perfect title

- **Outsource your way to an irresistible cover that readers love**

- Write your first draft – fast!

- **Block out distractions using must-have apps for any writer**

- Use the Pomodoro technique and stream of consciousness writing to triple your productivity

- **Edit and polish your first draft to make it shine**

- Hire a professional editor – without going broke

- **Use ninja techniques to find people to review your books on Amazon**

- Price your book to maximize long-term sales and income

- **Take advantage of Amazon's promotional tools to catapult your book to bestseller status**

Not only that, you will also receive the **exact templates and emails** I used to get people to review, market and promote my books.

WHO AM I?

With so many books on "how to write a book", why should you listen to me? Who am I?

My name is Akash Karia and I've been making a very healthy passive income as an author for the past two years. I have published over sixteen books on Amazon at the time of this writing (check out my author page here: www.bit.ly/AkashKaria) and consistently sell close to 100 books a day on Amazon alone.

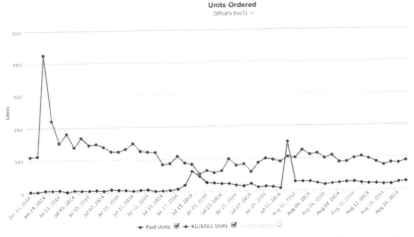

However, I'm NOT a full-time writer (despite the fact that I make more from publishing Kindle books than I do from my day job) because I love my day-job too much. I work as the Chief Commercial Officer for a multi-million dollar company in

Tanzania, and I enjoy the work too much to give it up – but I love writing too, so I balance both the careers that I have.

I don't say this to impress you, but to impress upon you that it is possible to keep your day job (if you choose to do so) AND still make a healthy passive income as an author. Even if you're busy, have never written a book before and don't have any experience in internet marketing, you can still profit from your words – as long as you have a burning desire to do so.

In this guide, I will share with you the process I use to quickly write high-quality non-fiction Kindle eBooks that sell. The process I share will help you cut years off your learning curve and help you write faster, sell more and profit quicker! I'm not saying it'll be an easy journey, but it'll be one that's worth it.

If you're ready, then let's get started...

Chapter Two

HOW TO PICK THE BEST NICHE TO MAXIMIZE YOUR SALES

~

DAY 1: CHOOSING YOUR NICHE

So, you want to write a book?

No, wait - you want to write a bestselling book?

The good news is that it's easier now than ever before to write, publish and make money from your words. How do I know? Because I've been making a great living as a self-published author for the last two years.

I don't have any special connections — I'm not a celebrity, nor do I have big agents or publishing houses marketing my work for me — but I have been able to use the power of self-publishing to write and publish over a dozen bestselling books that provide me with a steady stream of passive income.

In this book, I will teach you everything I know to help you write, publish and profit from your work in just 15 days!

What Is a Niche?

The very first thing you need to do is to choose your niche. A niche is just a specific topic about which you want to write. It helps if you choose a niche that you enjoy and for which you have passion.

When it comes to writing, the more passion and knowledge you have about a topic, the easier the words will flow. You'll have less research to do and you can fill the pages with all of your good ideas.

Some examples of topics that I enjoy writing about include:

- Public speaking
- Weight loss motivation
- Anti-procrastination techniques for writers
- Relationship issues

You can write about any topic you like. But before you can really begin to create a book you need to understand the basic niche that works for you. Writing a book can help you become an authority on whichever topic you choose.

This can branch off into other business areas within the same niche such as selling products, teaching courses, and creating a brand. This is another reason why you want to choose wisely – this could become a huge part of your working life.

How to Choose a Niche

You may already know exactly what you want to write about, but if you're not sure, there are a few things you can do to help you determine the best niche for you. Ask yourself a few key questions such as:

- Is there a topic on which I have a lot of knowledge?
- On what am I an expert?
- What topic or topics hold my interest?
- What could I research and present a "best of" to my readers?
- Are there any experts to whom I have access?

In my own life and experience, I know a lot about public speaking. As a result I've been able to write five best-selling books on it (www.bit.ly/AkashKaria).

The internet marketer Tim Ferris knows a tremendous amount about outsourcing and building passive income. As a result he wrote about it in the book *The 4-Hour Work Week*. It's always best if you can write on a topic that really fits your expertise. But maybe you don't feel like an expert on any subject. In that case, you have options.

One option is to become an expert in a topic that really interests you. If you're interested in something you'll be more motivated to research it and share your exciting discoveries.

For example, I'm very interested in success so I researched it and have been able to share what I've learned. I read academic literature on success and followed that research by writing a book

called *How Successful People Think Differently*
(www.bit.ly/SuccessUS). The book has proven to be highly
popular and has 49 reviews with an average rating of 4.5 stars
(out of five), which just goes to show you that as long as you
write a well-researched book, people will buy it and find value in
it.

Through the process of research you can become an expert on
just about any topic. But you can also use resources such as
experts in the field. Today's social media makes it easier to reach
out to experts.

You might want to interview a few experts in a particular niche
and then distill their wisdom into bite-sized chunks for your
readers. That's just what Napoleon Hill did in his book *Think and
Grow Rich*.

If you have access to experts in a particular niche, that can guide your selection of topics. But if you don't have immediate access to experts, don't let that stop you from trying to get in touch with experts in a field that interests you.

Above all, focus on writing a book that you'd be interested in reading. If you aren't interested in the book you're writing, your readers probably won't enjoy reading it either.

Is There a Demand?

Once you've chosen a niche, it's important to see if there's a demand for it before going forward. You can do several things to evaluate the marketplace and determine whether or not your book will be received favorably.

First, you can go to Amazon and search for titles on your topic. For example, if you want to write on public speaking, you'll type "public speaking" in the search bar. Browse the category and look for a few indicators.

How popular are the books in this category? You can tell by looking at the sales rank. You want to look for books that have a sales rank of 25,000 or less. The lower the number, the higher the sales of the book.

For example, at the time of this writing, the sales rank of one of my most popular books, *Storytelling Techniques from TED Talks* is 9,697 (www.bit.ly/TEDStorytelling). This book sells 200 to 300 copies every month and is currently the #2 best-selling guide in the Communication category.

If you can't find at least three books with that low sales rank, it means there isn't much demand for your topic. Let's look at the example of procrastination as a niche. If I wanted to write a book to help people fight procrastination, I would check with Amazon for books on procrastination.

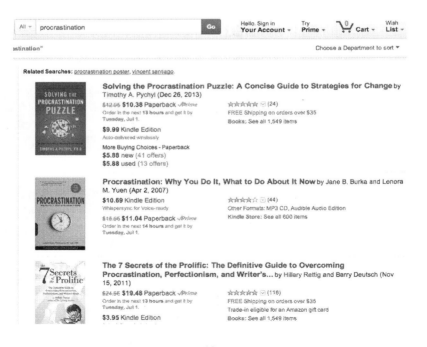

If I find that there are at least three books with a rank lower than 25,000, I can be sure that there's a demand for this topic.

If you're able to write a good book and market it well, you will make money. For example, at the time of this writing, I can see that *23 Anti-Procrastination Habits* by Steve Scott has a sales rank of 4,841. The book *Stop Procrastinating: 10 Power Habits* by Benjamin Wilson has a sales rank of 7,251. And my book, *Ready, Set... PROCRASTINATE: 23 Anti-Procrastination Tools* (www.bit.ly/AntiProcrastination) has a sales rank of 18,253. There are a lot more books on the topic of procrastination, which tells me that this is a topic that has sufficient demand.

If we look at the example of "pet grooming" as a niche we'll see something quite different. When you search for books on pet grooming you'll find that there aren't any in the top 25,000. The average sales rank for a book on pet grooming seems to hover around 200,000 (which is a terrible sales rank!).

Even if pet grooming is your passion, it might not be the best niche because it just won't sell. There's not enough demand. Even if you write a good book, you might not make much money on it.

If this happens, go back to Amazon and start researching Amazon Kindle books. You'll begin to see which topics sell well and which don't. You want to find topics that are selling well and that match up with your interests.

Udemy (www.udemy.com) is another resource to help you understand more about what's in demand. Udemy is a site that offers online learning courses. Currently the platform has over 8,000 courses created by 4,000 independent course creators.

If you go to Udemy you can browse through the categories and see what's popular. For example, go to the Business category and sort by "Popularity." This will show you the most popular business courses on the platform.

When I go to Udemy now and do this search, I see a course called "Body Language for Entrepreneurs." This course is selling for $199 and has over 1,100 students. This tells me there is a high demand because a lot of people are willing to pay a lot of money for this course. Yes, some of those students might have received free coupons for the course, but I'm betting that there are many who paid the full price.

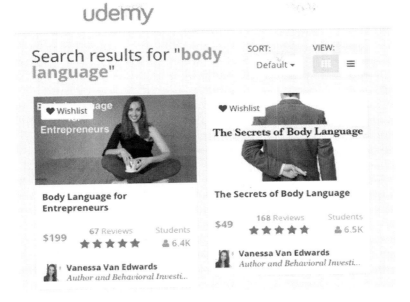

If I go back over to Amazon and perform a search for "body language" I see several Kindle titles including:

- *What Every BODY Is Saying* by Joe Navarro – selling at $9.99 and ranked 3,861 in the Kindle Store

- *The Definitive Book of Body Language* by Allan Pease – selling at $12.99 and ranked 14,115 in the Kindle Store

- *Body Language 101: The Ultimate Guide to Knowing When People Are Lying, How They Are Feeling, What They Are Thinking, and More* by David Lambert – selling at $0.99 and ranked 20,404 in the Kindle Store

So as you can see, at least three books are ranked below 25,000 in this category. This is another indication that "body language" is a popular topic. One interesting thing to note is that the third book, *Body Language 101,* has a terrible cover (no offense to the author) and an average of only three out of five stars in the reviews.

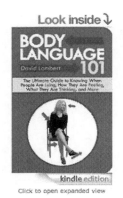

Look inside ↓

Body Language 101: The Ultimate Guide to Knowing When People Are Lying, How They Are Feeling, What They Are Thinking, and More [Kindle Edition]
David Lambert (Author)
★★★☆☆ (44 customer reviews)

Pricing information not available.

- Length: 196 pages (Contains Real Page Numbers)
- Optimized for larger screens
- Due to its large file size, this book may take longer to download
- Don't have a Kindle? Get your Kindle here.

Formats	Amazon Price	New from	Used from
Paperback	$11.66	$4.05	$2.30

Click to open expanded view

But it's still selling a decent number of copies, which proves that this is a profitable topic. Imagine what could happen if you have a great cover and quality content. Your book should be able to rank even higher. That means it can be very profitable for you.

Narrowing Your Niche

Now that you've done a little homework and researched the niche about which you're interested in writing, you need to narrow your topic down. Let's take a look at what that means and why it's important.

Someone new to writing on Kindle might decide to write a book called *How to Start a Business.* This topic is very popular, but it's far too wide. There are a few problems with this type of book.

First, there are already a lot of "how to start a business" books on Amazon. Yours won't seem any different if you go with that title. Why would anyone buy your book as opposed to one that has been published by a big-five publishing house with a famous author?

Second, this topic would take a long time to research and write properly. It could take you hundreds of hours and hundreds of pages to cover everything. And the price point for Kindle books is usually between $2.99 and $5.99. That would be a lot of work to do for such a little profit.

Finally, this title promises the readers too much. It's such a broad topic that the readers believe it will be the ultimate guide for any business. When they download the book they already will have very high expectations.

There will inevitably be things that you didn't cover in your guide and this will lead to disappointment – and bad reviews. And as a result of bad reviews, sales figures will plummet.

To prevent this disaster, you need to narrow your niche. You'll want to pick just ONE problem that your book can solve. It needs to be very clear and laser-targeted in order to make your readers happy.

For example, look at this book that you've just purchased. It's not a book on *How to Publish a Book*. Instead, it's *How to Write a Non-Fiction Kindle eBook in 15 Days*. As you can see, this is a very specific guide and has a specific target market including:

- Kindle writers
- Non-fiction book writers
- People interested in writing a book quickly

This does rule out a lot of people such as those who don't publish on Kindle, fiction writers, and those who don't agree that a book written in 15 days can be of high quality. But that's actually a good thing!

I find that only the right readers buy my books. That means I have a lower risk of negative reviews from a harsh reader who expected something different. It also helps my book to stand out from the competition.

My book automatically draws the readers who would be interested in it by not being so generic. And because I've focused on solving only one or two problems in my book I don't need to write hundreds of pages on the topic.

My book will be more focused and it will be shorter, making it a better option to price it at $2.99. Now if I write two or three of these shorter books, I can put them together in a bundle and sell them at a larger price.

For example, I have three books on the topic of writing:

- *How to Write a Non-Fiction Kindle eBook in 15 Days*
- *Anti-Procrastination Techniques for Writers*
- *How to Effortlessly Write 1000+ Words - Per HOUR: The 1K+ Writing System for Writing Nonfiction Books Faster!*

Each one of these titles focuses on a specific problem or challenge that writers face. I can sell each one of them individually at $2.99 and I can also bundle all three of them together and price it at $5.99.

This allows my dedicated followers to get a great discount on the package. It makes it easier for my readers to know what they're getting and find value in the books. For me it means more money than if I just wrote one big book on *How to Publish a Book*.

Day 1: Niche Task

Now that you have read through this chapter you may feel your own wheels starting to turn. Your task list for today, Day 1, is to determine your niche. You need to make sure that you:

- Choose a niche that interests you
- Research the demand for your niche
- Narrow down your niche so that your book is extremely focused on just one problem or challenge you can solve

Take this first day to make sure you have a niche that's in demand and that has the possibility of being profitable. Avoid the temptation to be too broad – do your best to be very specific for your readers. This first step will determine much of your success.

Chapter Three

SAY GOODBYE TO WRITER'S BLOCK ONCE AND FOR ALL

~

DAYS 2 – 4: DO YOUR RESEARCH

You've started by doing some research on the best niche for you. But now it's time to move onto the next step of researching your book. During this step you'll be gathering all the information that you need to create your masterpiece.

Avoid Blank Page Syndrome

Many people choose a niche and then just get started with writing. In fact, you may be so excited that you go on and write the first chapter. There's nothing inherently wrong with this, but if you don't do your research you can end up with "blank page syndrome" after chapter one.

What is blank page syndrome? Just about every writer has had it. You find yourself staring at a blank screen with absolutely nothing to write. Has this ever happened to you? This step of research is here to keep you from suffering from this syndrome.

If you were writing a fiction novel, it would require that you be creative and imaginative. It would only be natural to need time to consider what goes on each page. But with non-fiction writing, you end up with writer's block because you don't know *what* to write next, not because your imagination has left the building.

Thorough research before writing can save a lot of time by helping you to avoid blank page syndrome. When you know a lot about a subject and have plenty of material from which to draw, the writing process goes much more smoothly.

But I'm Already an Expert...

You probably chose your niche based on your interests and passion. In fact, you may already consider yourself a true expert – and you probably are! But that isn't always enough when it comes to writing a book.

I've made the mistake of skipping research myself. When I was writing my book titled *Persuasion Psychology: 26 Ways to Persuade Anyone to Do Anything* (www.bit.ly/PersuasionUS), I already had a strong grasp of the subject.

I had been doing my research and reading books on the topic for several years. However, I hadn't actually compiled all of my research into one place. After a couple of hours of writing, I realized I was stuck. I didn't know what to say next.

Of course, I blamed writer's block for my troubles. But the truth is that non-fiction writers should never face writer's block. If you do your research, you'll always know exactly what to say.

For this type of writing you don't need imaginative and flowery language. You just need to get your point across in the shortest, simplest way possible. Your reader wants to learn something new in a way that's easily and quickly understood.

Being an expert is wonderful and will make the writing process more enjoyable for you. But your book can always be improved with research. You might uncover new information that enhances the quality of your book.

If you're already an expert, though, you may not need to spend as much time on research as someone new to the subject. Even though you may need less time, you should still go ahead and do some research before jumping into the writing process.

Avoid Research While Writing

After struggling with my own book on persuasion, I stopped writing and went online to do some research. Once I gathered some new information, I went right back to writing. Before long, I was stuck again and had to go back and do more research.

The problem with this approach of researching while you write is that it breaks your flow of both research and writing. It makes both processes take longer.

When you write, you get into a rhythm and flow where the words just pour out of you. You are in the zone. You can write at a rapid pace because you've gotten into your topic and you know exactly what to say.

But when you have to start and stop to go back to finding and checking facts, you break this state of flow. Getting back to it can be very difficult. The same is true for research.

You get into a flow of finding information you need, moving from one site to another or reading great information in books. But when you stop and start, you have to remember where you were searching and it can be hard to get back into the flow of research.

It's always best to do as much research as you can ahead of time so that you don't succumb to the inefficient process of researching while writing. You'll find that when you do this you'll be able to research and write much faster.

Should You Write on This Topic?

Researching ahead of time also helps you to know for sure that you have a good topic for your book. You may find after some research that you don't really like the topic. It's much better to find out before you've spent a lot of time writing.

I've had some author friends who chose their niche and then immediately dove into the writing process. But before long they discovered that they didn't actually like the topic. In the end, they abandoned their book but not without investing a substantial amount of time in the writing process.

Doing research ahead of time can help you to avoid this. You may spend a day or two on research and then decide that this topic isn't for you after all. But if you write a few chapters and then discover that this isn't a great topic for you, you'll waste much more time.

During this phase of research, you'll be able to quickly deduce whether or not you should continue pursuing this book. And you won't feel any pressure to keep going because you've invested minimal time.

The Power of Research

Researching sounds simple, but don't underestimate its power. Research leads to:

- More knowledge
- Added interest for you and the reader
- A more information-rich book
- Better structure and organization in your writing
- Better customer reviews
- Improved sales

As you research you may also discover there's a wealth of information – so much you can't put it all in one book. This can help you to get content ready for a second, follow-up book on the topic.

Research can only make your book better. Sometimes people look at research and think of it as a dreaded experience. But if you choose a niche you really enjoy, the research actually becomes quite fun.

Four Tools to Research Your Topic Like a Pro

Now that you know *why* you need to perform research, let's look at *how* to do it properly and efficiently. You may be wondering what good research looks like. What does it actually mean to do research? Don't worry – I'll help you to learn the basics.

When you research your book, you want to become immersed in the topic. You'll want to know what problems you can solve for your readers and what the experts are saying about your topic. Read on to learn many ways you can do this.

1 – Google Keywords

Google's Keyword Planning tool (www.adwords.google.com/KeywordPlanner) can help you to discover what readers are searching for related to your topic. Go to this planning tool and search for your niche topic.

You'll get a list of words and phrases that are being searched related to your topic. This gives you an idea of what your future readers are looking for. Copy a list of the words and phrases that are searched for the most.

public speaking

	Ad group ideas	Keyword ideas				

1 - 1

Keyword (by relevance)		Avg. monthly searches ?	Competition ?	Suggested bid ?
public speaking tips		12,100	Medium	HK$13.80
fear of public speaking		12,100	Low	HK$23.01
effective public speaking		880	Medium	HK$20.65
public speaking courses		3,600	High	HK$43.91
public speaking training		1,600	High	HK$29.45
public speaking skills		2,900	Medium	HK$9.79
public speaking course		1,300	High	HK$26.67

This list can help you to see what problems your readers are facing so that you can structure your book to answer them. This can help you to nail down the direction of your book and be a guiding principle for your work.

2 – Blog posts

You can learn a lot by reading what others have to say about your topic. One great resource is Technorati. This is a blog directory tool that will allow you to search using your topic and get a list of blogs that are related to it. (*Update:* Unfortunately, Technorati just killed its blog ranking system: www.bit.ly/Technocrati)

However, you can find excellent blogs using Alltop (www.alltop.com). This will also give you posts that are relevant to your topic.

There are thousands and thousands of blogs online, which can be overwhelming. These two tools can help narrow it down and make research easier.

3 – Podcasts

Podcasts are excellent resources for learning more about your niche. You can find them on iTunes (www.apple.com/itunes) by searching keywords related to your niche. Then subscribe to the ones that are relevant to you.

Downloading and listening to podcasts can help you to learn more information related to your niche and give you more source material for your own non-fiction book. You can take notes as you listen to create a great list of ideas.

4 – Most popular highlights of Kindle eBooks

Kindle eBooks are inexpensive and can be invaluable when it comes to research. This is one of my favorite techniques for delving deeper into my research topic.

You'll want to go to the Amazon Kindle Store and purchase several of the best-selling books in your niche. Start with 5-10 on your topic. As you read through each book, you'll want to take notes on what you find useful.

Another feature of Kindle is that you can look at the most popular highlights by readers. When you turn on this feature in Kindle, you'll see what other users have found helpful and you can make sure to take note of important ideas. This is one of the most under-utilized yet effective techniques to help you find content that resonates with your readers.

Learning from what's already out there can help you to pick up on the best tips you read and hear. You can gain a deeper understanding of your niche and become more of an expert than you already are.

You'll learn which ideas are most popular as you read and this will also identify some of your readers' common problems. Your job as the writer is to work to solve those problems in an informative way.

You'll be able to write much faster if you've done your research. As you write, you'll begin adding your own perspective and you'll provide a new twist on what's already out there. This makes your book stand out from the competition.

Keeping Track of Important Information

As you research, it's important to keep track of the information that you come across. It doesn't do any good to learn about something and then just forget about it or the source. It's a good idea at the very beginning of the research process to document your findings.

You'll need to have a place to record all of the good ideas you come across. For many people it works to have a single document in which you type notes and copy down ideas. Even if you don't think you'll use a specific idea, it's a good idea to record it.

Having too much information is a good problem – it can help you to have the source material for future projects.

It's also important to keep track of the places you've done your online research. When you take notes and copy down an idea, make sure that you also copy and paste the link where it came from.

If you want to cite the idea later, you'll be able to give proper credit without having to look for it all over again. This is a major time saver and will help you to be a more efficient writer during that phase of the project.

Days 2 – 4: Research Task

I'm assuming that you already have a good grasp of the topic that you've chosen – that's one of the important parts of choosing a niche on Day 1. So now I recommend that you spend three full days on research.

Days 2-4 should be focused completely on gathering information and researching your book. This step is crucial in helping you to write faster and produce a high-quality book that your readers will love!

Chapter Four

THE QUICK & EASY METHOD FOR OUTLINING YOUR BOOK

~

DAYS 2-5: CREATE AN OUTLINE

Creating an outline for your book is an essential task that's critical to complete before you start writing. You've probably noticed that this task corresponds with most of the research phase. That's because these two processes go hand in hand.

Why Create an Outline?

An outline is important to the writing process for a couple of different reasons. First, an outline helps you to know the structure and direction of your book. Ultimately, having an outline will help you to write faster.

When you have your outline completed before you begin writing, you'll be able to avoid blank page syndrome. When it's time to sit down at your desk to write your book, you'll never have to deal with writer's block.

With an outline you can know exactly what it is you want to write. And you can create a book that flows from topic to topic in an organized way that your readers will also appreciate.

For a long time I hated outlining my books. I thought that it was silly and a waste of time. I thought that I could dive straight into writing and let my ideas magically be transported from my head to the page. However, I quickly found out that didn't work as well as I expected.

The outline is a tool that acts like a bridge between your head and the page. The ideas are already in your head, but the outline can give you a clear, structured path to writing your ideas and creating a good book.

Outlining Made Simple

Your outline doesn't need to be a tedious task. In fact, you can quickly outline your book in a simple process. Here's how I do it:

Table of Contents

First, I create a new document titled "Outline." In this Word document, I create a Table of Contents and then I create sample chapter titles. For example, for this book I created the chapter titles "Choose Your Niche," "Do Your Research," and "Create an Outline."

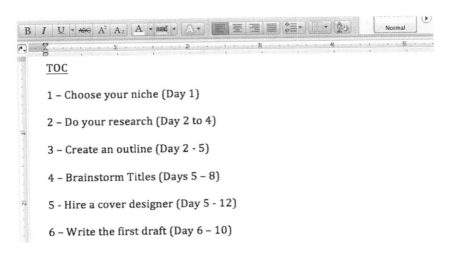

You'll notice I'm not trying to come up with fancy titles nor am I overthinking the process. I am simply brainstorming my possible chapter titles. Since most non-fiction books have a step-by-step logical process, your chapters will also follow that type of sequence.

After you've written your possible chapter titles, take a look at the Table of Contents and see if it makes logical sense. You may find that you need to move a few of them around so that the book flows nicely in a logical order.

Add main points

Once you have your table of contents fleshed out, you can add more information. For each chapter you'll want to add a few main points. In my own process I add in bullet points that are the three to six main points, stories, or examples I want to cover in that chapter.

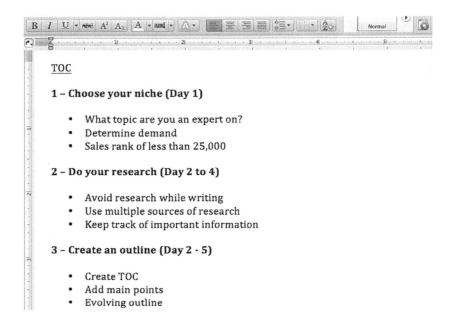

I don't worry about making a detailed outline. This is just a brief skeleton of the book that shows me what the overall book will cover. I can always know what to write next and I can keep the organization and flow of the book consistent. And that's it!

An evolving outline

One important thing to note is that as you write, your outline will evolve. The outlining portion takes place, in part, at the same time as your research phase. As you research and learn more information, your brain will be mentally creating an outline.

It makes sense, then, to go ahead and dump this information into a Word document, or at least write it down on paper. This way you don't have to remember what you want to add – it's already there for you in an outline form.

After you finish the research phase, though, you'll want to dedicate one day specifically to your outline. You'll want to ensure that your outline is complete and comprehensive. Before you begin writing, you should feel happy with what it will contain.

Days 2 – 5: Outline Task

For the first part of this time period, Days 2-4, you'll want to just start outlining your book as you research. You'll find that this saves a lot of time when it comes to writing your book.

On Day 5, though, you'll want to go over the outline one last time to make sure you're happy with it before you move on to the next step. Once you feel satisfied with your outline and you feel like you have everything you need in it, you can move on to the next task of selecting the perfect title.

Chapter Five

HOW TO CRAFT POWERFUL BOOK TITLES THAT GENERATE SALES

~

DAYS 5-7: TITLES

Now that you have your outline finished, you're probably ready to start writing. But wait! You're not quite there yet. Normally, with traditional publishing, that's what you'd do. However, with non-fiction Kindle books I recommend a different approach.

As a Kindle author you're responsible for everything in the publication process – from the writing to the editing to the cover design. That means there's a lot to think about while you're putting your book together.

With Kindle publishing, authors live in an exciting age where anyone can make money from their words – and I mean anyone. It's simply a matter of following the right steps that are recommended in this guide and then repeating them over and over with as many books as possible.

You might not earn hundreds of thousands of dollars per book, but each book can easily put a couple hundred extra dollars in your pocket each month. So the more books you produce over time, the higher your income will be.

Title Creation Saves Time

I am particularly interested in creating high quality eBooks in a short amount of time. Because of that, I've created a team of professional editors and designers who help me with my books.

I have a cover designer who designs excellent eBook covers for me. I'll share more about hiring a cover designer in the next chapter.

I also have a team of two editors who edit and help refine my books to ensure they read well. It's important to have an extra set of eyes to read your material – you see it so much that you may miss mistakes or things that make sense to you but would be confusing to someone else.

This help is invaluable, but each of these people will take a couple of days to complete the work I give them. So in order to speed up the process, I like to insure that I reduce the wait time to as short as possible.

By creating the book title before I start writing my book, I can then outsource it to my designer. This way, my cover designer can be coming up with new designs for the book while I start writing the book.

I used to wait until I was finished writing to come up with titles for my books. However, this added at least a week of waiting time for the cover to come back. After I finished the writing, I would spend at least a day brainstorming titles.

Then I would give the title to my designer and wait for up to a week while he developed the cover designs. Now, I can speed up the process by generating the title first. Of course, if speed isn't your primary concern you can wait until you've finished writing.

Developing THE Title

How long should it take to generate a title? Not long at all. It really shouldn't take more than a couple of hours. I prefer to start brainstorming my title on the day I finish the outline for my book.

This is a good time to brainstorm because you've already:

- Chosen your niche
- Checked out competition on Amazon
- Gathered the research
- Created an outline
- Determined the purpose of the book

From your research, you'll know what readers need and what benefits you can give them. All you need to do, then, is to create a title that lets your potential readers know that your book can solve their problems.

The Importance of a Great Title

If you want a best-selling book, you can't underestimate the power of the title. As an example, consider the story of Emanuel Hardeman-Julius.

Hardeman-Julius was an American author who published his works during the early 20th century. In just two decades, he sold more than 200 million books. If you consider the time period, you'll realize how successful he was.

But a lot of his success can be attributed to his book titles – and his distinctive way of testing them. He would actually publish the same books under different titles and determine which sold better.

For example, his book titled *The Mystery of the Iron Mask* sold approximately 11,000 copies a year. However, the same book with the title *The Mystery of the Man in the Iron Mask* was much more successful, selling over 30,000 copies in a single year.

Both of these books were identical stories. The only difference was the title – and that made all the difference when it came to sales. He had several successful title changes that brought success.

For example, his book *Casanova and His Loves* sold a respectable 8,000 copies. But when he changed the title to *Casanova, History's Greatest Lover* the book sold more than 22,000 copies.

One of the most successful title changes was for his book *Art of Controversy*. With this title it sold exactly zero copies in a year. But when he renamed it *How to Argue Logically*, it sold more than 30,000 copies. Again, same book, just a different title.

What Makes a Great Title?

There are several factors that can help to make your title great. Titles for non-fiction books should be relatively simple. Here's what you want:

- A title that is short
- A subtitle that clearly conveys the benefit of your book to your readers
- A title and subtitle that contain the keywords your Amazon readers would use when looking for books on your topic

Let's look at the process of developing your title in more detail. You want your main title to be 10 words or fewer. This isn't a hard and fast rule, but a guideline that I recommend. You can definitely create a title that is longer and have success.

But I find that a short title with a longer subtitle is the combination that works best on Amazon. There are two types of short titles that seem to do well: benefit titles and curiosity titles.

41

Benefit titles

The first type of title clearly identifies what the book is about and the benefits that readers can expect from it. I call these "benefit titles." The following are some examples that caught my eye and interested me enough to purchase them:

- *How to Win Friends and Influence People* by Dale Carnegie
- *50 Fitness Tips* by Derek Doepker
- *101 Ways to Start a Business for Less than $1000* by Tom Corson Knowles
- *Conquering Google Adsense* by Pablo Vici
- *How I Made Over $100,000 Online Doing What I Love* by Henri Juntilla
- *How to Sell Video Courses Online* by Rob Cubbon

And a couple of my own titles that follow this format include:

- *How to Deliver a Great TED Talk* by Akash Karia
- *Anti-Procrastination for Writers* by Akash Karia

Notice that each of these titles is very simple and straightforward. By reading them you can tell exactly what you'll get. They promise you, the reader, what knowledge you'll receive and how it will benefit you. I like these types of titles and they have been working very well for me.

When you're writing your own title, you need to ask yourself:

What does this book offer my readers? What problem does it help them to solve? What will reading this book allow the reader to accomplish?

Then, in less than 10 words, create a title that clearly and simply demonstrates this. Here are a few title templates to help you get started:

- **How to** (add benefit here: e.g., "Write Non Fiction eBooks in 15 Days")
- **How to** (add benefit here: e.g., "Lose Weight Quickly") **Without** (add pain here: e.g., "Having to Diet")
- **23 Ways to** (add benefit here: e.g., "Promote Your Non-Fiction eBook Online")
- **10 Days to** (add benefit here: e.g., "A Swimsuit Body")
- **How I** (add your success story: e.g., "Raised Myself from Success to Failure in Sales")

These are just a few examples for creating your own eBook title. The important thing is that if you go with this type of title, it needs to be clear, straightforward, and promise your reader something of value.

Curiosity titles

The second type of titles is curiosity titles. These make you wonder about something and pique your interest. Some good examples include:

- *Becoming the 1%* by Dennis Crosby (Makes you wonder, "Becoming the 1%? What does that mean?")
- *E-Squared* by Pam Grout (Makes you wonder, "Hmm, what's that about?")
- *Hooked* by Nir Eyal (Makes you wonder, "Hooked to what?")

While such titles can arouse reader curiosity, on their own they can be confusing. To be effective, they need to have benefit-driven subtitles. The title grabs your attention, but the subtitle tells you what the book is really about.

Here are the full titles of the books mentioned above so you can see what I mean:

- *Becoming the 1%: How to Master Time Management and Rise to the Top in 7 Days* by Dennis Crosby
- *E-Squared: Nine Do-It-Yourself Energy Experiments That Prove Your Thoughts Create Your Reality* by Pam Grout
- *Hooked: How to Build Habit-Forming Products* by Nir Eyal

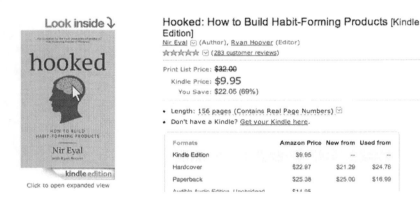

If you go with a curiosity title, it should be very short so that you can include a longer, benefit-laden subtitle. This helps your ideal reader to find your book and want to explore it further. While the main title piques curiosity, it's the subtitle that clearly communicates what the reader is going to find in the book.

Giving Readers the Benefits They Want

Providing your readers with benefits is critical to the success of your Kindle book. It's important, then, to understand what types of benefits readers are generally looking for from an eBook.

There are actually four types of general benefits or promises that will entice readers to purchase your book. They make up the acronym EDGE (**E**steem more, **D**o more, **G**ain more, **E**njoy more). This great information comes from Craig Valentine's book, *World Class Speaking*.

E – Esteem more

These are benefits that will help your readers to have more esteem. They may want to develop more confidence, learn to be more assertive, or overcome shyness.

D – Do more

This type of benefit allows your readers to do more. For example, they may want to become more productive in their work. Titles that include messages such as "double your productivity" or "triple your reading speed" appeal to this type of benefit.

G – Gain more

This type of benefit allows readers to gain more in any area of life. For example, they may "gain more money," "gain more time," or "gain more friends."

E – Enjoy more

Benefits that help your readers to enjoy their life more are very appealing. For example, a book could teach "how to stop negative thinking and lead a happier life."

When it comes to your own book, which one of these benefits will motivate your readers? There could be more than one. Be sure that your title or subtitle includes this benefit. Why?

Because readers don't buy non-fiction books to read; they buy non-fiction books because of the benefits and value that they will gain. If your book offers readers a clear and compelling benefit, they'll be more likely to buy it.

Brainstorming Your Own Book Title

Now that you've learned a bit about what makes a best-selling title, it's time to start working on your own title. Here's what I recommend you do:

Know your audience

Think carefully about who your ideal readers are. What is their #1 pain point? What problem are they looking to solve? What benefit does your book offer them? Why would they buy your book?

Create a spider map

After you've really spent time thinking about your audience, grab a piece of paper and write the word "Title" in the middle of the page. Circle that word. This makes up the "body" of your spider.

Now start creating your spider's "legs" by writing down as many possible titles as you can, branching off from your circle. Spend 30 minutes doing this. Don't worry about whether or not your ideas are good.

This isn't a time to judge your ideas – that will actually stop the flow of creativity. At this point, no idea is a bad one. At the end of 30 minutes you can choose the one you think works best. Or you may find that putting a couple of ideas together works well.

Have a title party

If you're still in need of a great title, you can have a title party. Invite as many friends as you can over for dinner. It's great if they're in your target audience, but they certainly don't have to be for this to work.

Have pizza and drinks, or whatever your friends like. Then take 30 minutes to let everyone know what your book is about and ask them to help you generate some ideas for titles.

Ask people to shout out their answers and write them down on a large piece of paper. Again, don't judge the ideas, just write them down. This gives you more options. After the half hour, you can go back to your social occasion with your friends.

Testing Your Title

Now that you've done some brainstorming and narrowed down your favorite titles, it's time to test and choose a title. There are several ways you can do this before you make your final decision.

Facebook/Twitter votes

One way of testing your titles is through social media. Social media gives us a great way of testing titles with a large group of people. My process is to post the titles on my Facebook page or through Twitter.

Then I ask my friends which titles they like best. I also do this when choosing book cover designs. The likes and comments that I get help me to know my friends' opinions and this gives me an outsider's perspective.

There have even been occasions when my friends have come up with better titles than the ones I thought of. This is a great way to broaden my choices.

Facebook/LinkedIn ads

I love to get the opinions of my friends, but I also want to have some concrete evidence about which title gets the highest click-through rates. How do I do this? I use Facebook and LinkedIn ads. Let me walk you through the general process.

1. Create an ad

You'll go to Facebook or LinkedIn to set up and create an ad. If you haven't set up a Facebook ad before, this link will walk you through the process better than I can: www.facebook.com/advertising/faq

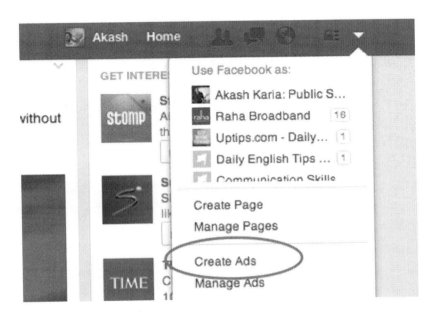

For LinkedIn, this is a good link to walk you through the process: www.linkedin.com/ads

2. Create several versions of the same ad

Everything about the ads should be the same — how much money you spend, the target audience, the images, etc. — with the exception of the title text. You want to really narrow down this variable that's being tested.

For example, if you're trying to decide between two titles for your book, you'll set up two identical ads except the text for one ad will be one of your proposed book titles and the second ad will be for the other proposed book title.

3. Select your target market for the ad
Both Facebook and LinkedIn allow you to choose your target audience. You need to take advantage of this and select the audience that's most likely to buy your book.

For example, if I were publishing a book on public speaking my target audience would be:

- People living in the USA, because that's where most of my eBook sales are generated.
- Between the ages of 22 and 40, because I'm targeting working professionals.
- Interested in "public speaking" (on Facebook you can choose according to interest).

4. Select a budget and bid range for both ads
I usually select a budget of $10 per ad and select the "pay-per-click" option. This means you pay only when someone clicks on your ad. The other option is "pay-for-impressions" where you pay for each 1,000 impressions of your ad, regardless of how many people click on it. Generally, I avoid this option because I personally haven't seen good results from it (although that isn't to say that you won't).

Both Facebook and LinkedIn will give me their suggested bid ranges per click. This means how much I should pay per click. I usually choose the minimum bid per click for my target market.

Your minimum bid rate will be different depending on who you are targeting. I usually find that choosing the minimum rate works well enough, though I sometimes adjust the bid upwards if I find that the ad isn't being shown frequently enough.

5. Run the ads for a day and evaluate results
After I run the ads, I come back the next day and monitor the two ads. You can get many statistics for each of your ads, including the number of impressions each ad generated and how many clicks each ad received.

Both Facebook and LinkedIn will give you a "click-through" rate. This shows you what percentage of the people who saw the ad actually clicked it. The higher the click-through rate, the better the title is. Please note that you won't actually be selling any books with these ads – the point is simply to see which ad gets clicked on more so that you can make a decision regarding the title of your book!

Email subject line A/B testing

The third method I like to use for testing book titles is A/B testing. I run two popular blogs, www.AkashKaria.com and www.CommunicationSkillsTips.com. I encourage people who visit my blog to subscribe to my email list so they can receive free updates as well as discounted offers.

To entice them to give me their email address, I offer some high-quality, free eBooks they can download once they subscribe. These opt-in books motivate people to join my list, and the quality of the books helps to create a loyal following.

Subscribe to our mailing list

Email Address *

First Name

SUBSCRIBE

Building an email list is critical because it allows you to build a fan base. We'll talk more about this later. If you're already a savvy author and have built an email list, you can perform this test. If not, you'll want to start creating an email list to use in the future. (I'll teach you how to build your own email list in Chapter 7.)

If you do have a list, though, and you're considering two different titles, you can perform a test with your list. For example, let's say I was considering writing an eBook on how to publish a book on Amazon. I have two potential titles for the book:

A – How to Write a Non-Fiction Kindle eBook in 15 Days
B – 15 Days to a Best-Selling Non-Fiction Kindle eBook

You can run an email test to see which one of these does better with your list of loyal followers. Here are the step-by-step instructions for doing this.

1. **Log in to your email delivery platform**. I currently use MailChimp (www.mailchimp.com), but you can also do this with other email delivery platforms such as Aweber (www.aweber.com) and ConstantContact (www.constantcontact.com).

2. **Create a "new campaign" to send to your list**.

3. **Choose the A/B Split Testing Option**. Then select "A/B Testing via Subject Line." A/B Testing is very simple. You'll basically be sending two versions of the same email (version A and version B) to your list. The emails will be identical except for the two different titles in the subject line.

4. For the question, "What would you like to test?" **select the option "Subject lines."**

5. **Enter the two email titles in the A/B subject line split.**

6. The next step is to **write the body of the email**. This will be the same for both versions of the email – and your email delivery client will take care of making sure that happens.

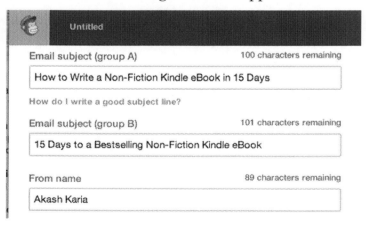

You can't send out a blank email! So, you need to come up with something to share with your followers. I like to write a blog post on the topic. For this example, I might write a short blog post titled "Writing a Non-Fiction Kindle eBook in 15 Days."

I will include the steps to writing an eBook in 15 days, but they won't be detailed the way this eBook is. But they will be valuable enough for my readers to feel they've gotten a benefit by reading them.

At the end of the post, I'll add a short promotional sentence. For example, "If you enjoyed this post, then watch for my upcoming eBook on how to publish a best-selling Kindle eBook in 15 days – where I reveal the exact system I used to publish 12 #1 best-selling books in one year while keeping my day job!"

This helps to build some buzz for my new book so that people on my list are ready to buy it when it's published.

5. **Send the email to your list.** Your email client will send half of your list with version A in the subject line and the other half will receive version B. This is done with random selection.

6. **Monitor the open rates for the email.** Within the next two days you'll be able to see which version of the email was opened most. The one that was opened most is going to be a more popular title that grabs readers' attention.

Your Choice Doesn't Have to Be Permanent

After following one or all of these testing suggestions, it will be clear which title is performing the best and will work best for your Kindle book. It's time now to commit to a title so that you can send it to your cover designer. This way the cover will be ready when you're finished writing and you can publish right away.

Some people truly agonize over a book title. If you find that you still want to change it – even after you publish it – you can. One of the great things about Kindle is that you can always change your book title.

You may find that after your book has been published for a few months, you come up with a better title. All you have to do is go to the editing panel of the Kindle publishing dashboard and you can change the title.

For example, the first book I published was titled *Speak Like a Winner*. However, the book wasn't doing as well as I hoped. It did promise readers value, but the title was too vague and didn't contain the main keyword which was "public speaking."

So, I changed the book title to *Public Speaking Mastery* (www.bit.ly/SpeakingMasteryUS). I also had to change the cover, but that only cost $5 so it wasn't a huge investment.

PUBLIC SPEAKING MASTERY - Speak Like a Winner: Public Speaking Techniques to Make You Twice the Speaker in Half the Time [Kindle Edition]
Akash Karia ⊡ (Author)
★★★★⯪ ⊡ (26 customer reviews)

Kindle Price: $2.99 ✓Prime

kindleunlimited   Read this title for free and get unlimited access to over 700,000 titles. Learn More
Prime members can borrow this book and read it on their devices with Kindle Owners Lending Library.

- Length: 136 pages (estimated) ⊡
- Word Wise: Enabled ⊡

After I made that change, the book sales began to rise within two weeks!

One important tip: When changing your Amazon book page, only change one thing at a time. You want to isolate which variable caused the change in sales. For example, if you change the book title, don't change anything else. If you change the book description, don't change anything else.

Changing variables one at a time will help you to know which one caused the sales change. This is important when you're marketing future volumes. You'll want to have at least two weeks between any changes to see if your change resulted in an increase or decrease in sales.

Days 5 – 7: Title Tasks

During this time period, you need to:

- Make sure you know your audience. What problems are they searching for? What benefit can you give them?
- Brainstorm titles
- Narrow down your titles to no more than two
- Test your titles
- Commit to a title

Performing this process now will allow you to have a cover created ahead of time so that you're ready to publish when the writing is done. And remember, you can always change your cover later if you find that there's one that would work better. For now, go ahead and commit to one so that you can be efficient with this process.

Chapter Six

OUTSOURCE YOUR WAY TO AN IRRESISTIBLE COVER THAT READERS LOVE

~

DAYS 6 – 12: HIRE A COVER DESIGNER

Once you have a title for your eBook, it's time to hire a cover designer. You want a cover that will have an eye-catching and sexy design. For that you'll need a professional to get the job done right.

The book cover is one of the most important parts of your book. My book *Anti Negativity* (www.bit.ly/AntiNegativityUS) had poor sales and was selling an average of only one copy per day. I had already changed the title from *Stop Negative Thinking: What Not to Say When You Talk to Yourself* to *Anti Negativity: How to Stop Negative Thinking, Eliminate Limiting Beliefs & Lead a Positive Life.*

But even with that change, there had been only a minimal sales increase. I decided, then, to change the cover. The old cover looked like this:

The new cover looks like this:

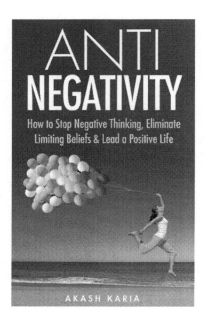

The results? Immediately after the cover change the book went from being #80 in its category to being a #1 bestseller in its category! Over the past couple of months it's gone from selling an average of one book per day to selling three books per day.

No matter what anyone says, people do judge a book by its cover!

Don't Do It Yourself!

Many people try to design their own covers for their books. But since the cover is so important, don't design it yourself if you're not a professional graphic designer. Believe me, I tried designing my own book covers and they sucked.

The crappy looking covers I designed resulted in an income loss for me. So just start from the beginning by investing in a great-looking cover – it will quickly pay for itself.

If you peruse Amazon and look through eBook covers you'll be able to tell which ones are homemade and amateur and which ones are professionally made. There's a huge difference – and buyers are drawn to quality and professional looking books.

What Makes a Great Cover?

Now that you know how important a cover is, you may be wondering what makes a great cover. There are several things that make a great cover and you need to make sure your cover has these attributes.

Title. First, the title should be large and readable in its thumbnail version on Amazon. The thumbnail image is the most commonly seen on Amazon. Your book will appear as a thumbnail on the "Customers also bought" section of your competitors' books.

Customers Who Bought This Item Also Bought

TED Talks Storytelling: 23 Storytelling...	Own the Room: Presentation...	The Storytelling Method: Steps To Maximize a...	How to Design TED Worthy Presentation Slides:...	PUBLIC SPEAKING MASTERY - Speak...
› Akash Karia	› Akash Karia	› Matt Morris	› Akash Karia	› Akash Karia
★ ★ ★ ★ ☆ 40	★ ★ ★ ★ ★ 22	★ ★ ★ ★ ★ 23	★ ★ ★ ★ ☆ 39	★ ★ ★ ★ ☆ 26
Kindle Edition	Kindle Edition	Kindle Edition	Kindle Edition	Kindle Edition
$2.99	$2.99	$4.99	$6.49	$2.99

You want to make sure the thumbnail of your cover looks great enough that readers click on it. They should be able to read the title (or at least the most important keyword) even on that tiny image.

Contrast. In order for your cover to be readable, you need to use contrasting colors for the background, text, and images. This clear color distinction makes it easier for the eye to distinguish the title and image. Here's an example of one of my book covers with great contrast (www.bit.ly/Magnetic-Speaking):

Simplicity. You want your book title to be clutter-free and simple. It needs to be easy on the eyes and look professional. If there's too much jumbled on the cover, it's hard for the reader to quickly scan and find the title and information. Less is more for your cover.

Where to Get a Great Cover

You know you need a great cover, but you may not know where to find a good designer. Never fear – I have many resources for you. There are several places where you can get great designers. Read on for my favorites.

Fiverr

Fiverr is a site where you can hire people to do all sorts of work for you for only $5. You can get some exceptional work on

Fiverr if you know where to look. There are many great eBook designers working full-time on Fiverr.

That said, if you're going to use Fiverr, you need to know how to get the most from it. This is the process I recommend:

1. First, **go to Fiverr** (www.fiverr.com) and search for "book cover designers" in the search bar.

2. Next, **filter them by "rating."** This will give you a list of the highest-rated cover designers, who have given great work in the past.

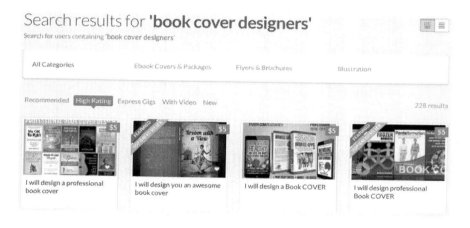

3. Then you need to **look at the real-work samples** for each designer – most designers have many samples. There are a lot of highly rated designers, but they're not always a good fit.

There were many I did not try out because I hated the samples of the book covers that they had displayed. If you don't like the samples, chances are you're not going to like the product you order.

4. **Go through as many of the Fiverr gigs as it takes** and decide on at least two people whose previous cover designs you like.

5. **Hire at least two Fiverr designers whose work you like**. You may also want to contact them before hiring to ask questions and explain what you want. Hiring two designers gives you the ability to see different concepts of how the cover can look. This allows you to choose the one that fits with your ideas the best.

6. When you hire designers, **send them each an email describing your expectations**. Be as specific as possible.

Because your cover design is so important for success, sometimes I like to get involved with the concept creation. For example, I search for images on Shutterstock.com and tell the designer which image I'd like used.

For example, for my book *Persuade Anyone* (www.bit.ly/PersuasionUS), I bought the image on Shutterstock (www.shutterstock.com) and told my designer (Fiverr Name: Akira) to use it. I did the same for my book on anti-procrastination for writers.

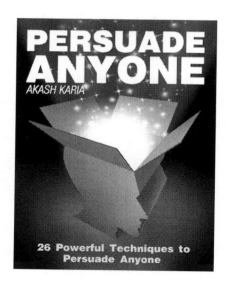

The covers look good and the final outcomes matched what I really wanted. How much control you want to have is up to you when it comes to your own book covers.

If you have a good eye for cover design, you may want to have more input. But if you feel that's not your forte, you can happily let your designer take the lead.

Elance

Another good place to find eBook cover designers is Elance (www.elance.com). To do this, it's very simple to create an Elance account and then post a new job. With Elance, you post a job and then designers have the opportunity to send proposals of what they'll do and how much they'll charge.

When you have proposals, you can then go through the profiles of all of the designers to look at samples. You can actually look at the profiles of any graphic designers. If you find one whose samples you like, you can invite them to bid.

One thing to note is that Elance is more expensive than Fiverr. The average book cover costs between $40 and $300. But you can get very good quality work there.

My first cover for the book *Speak Like a Winner* (which was later titled *Public Speaking Mastery*) was designed for $50 by a designer whom I found on Elance.

The cover for my next book, *How to Deliver a Great Ted Talk* (www.bit.ly/GreatTED) was designed by Adrian Stickney, whom I also found on Elance, for $60.

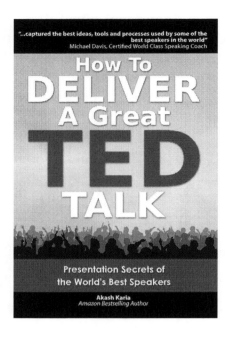

We went through more than 20 modifications on the cover before I finally settled on the final design, and all of that editing was included in the cost.

99Designs

Another route you can go with an eBook cover is to set up a contest on 99Designs (www.99designs.com). This allows you to get many different designs from designers who want to "win" the contest.

This is actually a more expensive option, but I know some authors who have had success with it. You get top-notch work and you'll have a huge number of choices in the end.

My friend, Maureen Zapalla, used this method and got a very good cover from it.

High Altitude Strategies picked a winning design in their book cover contest

For just $299, they received 63 designs from 13 designers.

Check out the designs she received here: www.bit.ly/99-covers

Tips for Working with Cover Designers

In general, I find investing a bit more time by hiring multiple designers on Elance and/or Fiverr usually gets the best results. In the end I get a very good job for a low price. If you're tight on funds, Fiverr can work out great and is very inexpensive.

But you need to be prepared to spend more time and be more involved with the process. You also need to be willing to hire more than one designer if the first one doesn't work out the way you had hoped.

No matter how you choose to hire cover designers, here are a few tips for making sure you get a cover you ultimately love.

It's OK to negotiate

Don't be afraid to negotiate with your cover designer. As long as you're willing to purchase more "gigs" or pay a little more, many designers will be willing to do extra work. You can get several extra cover designs to choose from this way.

Make sure your designer follows Amazon's specifications

It's important that your designer create a cover that meets Amazon's guidelines, otherwise your cover will get rejected. Be sure to send this link to your designer –www.bit.ly/Amazon-Instructions – because it contains Amazon's requirements. The most important requirement to keep in mind is the size requirement:

Requirements for the size of your cover art have an ideal height/width ratio of 1.6, which means:
• A minimum of 625 pixels on the shortest side and 1000 pixels on the longest side
• For best quality, your image would be 2820 pixels on the shortest side and 4500 pixels on the longest side

Don't settle

Don't settle for the first cover design that the designer gives you. Always ask for revisions. But when you ask for revisions, be specific. You need to share what you liked and what you want changed. At this point you may want to provide some samples as a reference so the designer can see what you want.

Remember that your cover is one of the most important parts of your book. It's important that you get a good look that you like. Ultimately, if you don't like the cover your designer gives you, it's a good idea to hire someone else.

You'll simply go through the same process until you're happy with the end result. Your cover should look like it was designed by a professional in a big-five publishing firm. It should look like something you could pick up at a retail bookstore.

Stick with a winner

When you do find a great designer, you'll want to stick with him or her in the future. Once you have a good working relationship with someone, you'll find that the process becomes simpler. When the designer knows what you like and don't like, you'll have to give less and less input to get what you want.

Testing Your Covers

Once you have a couple of different covers you like, you'll want to test them. You can use the same methods we discussed in the last chapter for testing titles. These options include:

- Posting covers on Facebook and asking for votes
- Creating Facebook and LinkedIn ads, changing only the image
- Trial and error – publishing your book and changing the cover if needed to boost sales

This will help you to arrive at the best cover for your book. You'll be able to have an attractive and compelling cover that increases sales.

Days 6 – 12: Cover Tasks

You'll be working on your cover design concurrently with your writing. Start by choosing a method for hiring a designer – Fiverr, Elance, or 99Designs. Go through profiles and find a designer with samples you like.

Then hire a couple of different designers to get some options for great covers. Work with those designers to get the cover exactly the way you like it. Then test the covers to choose the best one.

Chapter Seven

HOW TO WRITE YOUR FIRST DRAFT – FAST!

~

DAYS 6 - 12: WRITE THE FIRST DRAFT

You're finally to the part you've been looking forward to – writing your book! But that can be easier said than done. In this chapter I'll share with you some of the best techniques for writing your non-fiction book quickly and effectively.

When I first began writing on Kindle, I read books on how to write and publish Kindle books. Many of these books make writing a non-fiction book for Kindle seem like a linear process, but I have discovered that the opposite is true.

Writing Isn't a Linear Process

For example, the first day you gather your research, the next day you craft your outline, and the next day you create your title, then you begin writing your draft, etc. But what I found out is that writing isn't always so simple and straightforward.

The truth is that **writing is a messy, nonlinear process**. From my experience, you create your outline *while* you do your research. You start writing the first draft *while* you craft the title.

Some of these activities don't take entire days – for example, crafting a title is not a full-day activity. You might spend an hour brainstorming the first day and a couple of hours brainstorming the next day.

When you're not brainstorming, you have plenty of time to be writing your book. And when you're not writing or brainstorming, you can be finding the right cover designer and working with him or her to develop a fantastic cover.

I'm trying to show you my writing process and schedule so you'll see that the days you work on can skip around. It isn't necessary to do one task following another in a perfect sequential order.

In the previous chapter you were working on days 6-12 and in this chapter you're working on days 6-12. Since reading a book is much more linear than writing one, this may seem a bit confusing.

But don't worry – at the end of the book I will show you an outline that clarifies which activities I follow on specific days.

Writing Is Unique to You

Writing is a very individual process. You may follow this plan to the letter, but you may also find that shifting things around makes more sense for you. For example, you might decide to shift the title creation to the end. Or you might want to spend more time than I do on cover design.

It doesn't matter as long as you understand the main elements of this book and overall tasks that are required. This 15-day writing plan is not rigid.

By sharing my plan with you, I simply hope to inspire you with the assurance that writing a high-quality Kindle book is a straightforward process. With dedication, anyone can learn how to publish a high-quality Kindle book in just 15 days.

In this chapter, you'll learn techniques and tools that can help you write your first draft in just seven days. Read on for seven steps to writing your first draft.

1. Estimate your book length

First, you'll want to estimate the length of your book. Approximately how many words do you want it to contain? We've already talked about the benefits of shorter length eBooks.

If you've picked a small niche, you don't need your book to be all-encompassing. Instead of choosing to write about everything under the sun, you can be very specialized and keep the book short.

From my experience, my best-selling eBooks are also my shortest books. Generally speaking, most Kindle eBooks are between 12,000 and 30,000 words in length. I usually aim for 15,000 words and sell the book for $2.99.

At this price point I attract a lot of buyers who are willing to spend a few dollars just to find out what I have to say. At the same time I'm able to get across the main gist of information in 15,000 words. My readers actually appreciate my books being concise and direct.

I use 15,000 words as a general rule, but I can go over or under depending on how much information I want to convey. I often will add more information or cut something out when it doesn't seem to fit. But it's a good idea to come up with an estimate so that you can complete the next step.

2. Set a daily word-count goal

Since you have a goal of completing your book in seven days, you'll want to set a daily goal that gets you there. For a 15,000-word book you'll want to divide 15,000 by 7 to get 2,150 words per day.

Because you'll probably remove some portion of the book during the editing process, you may want to add an additional 10% to your daily goal. In this case, you'd up the number to about 2,400 words each day.

Post this number where you'll see it each day to remind you of your goal. A daily word count will help to keep you accountable and increase your motivation to reach your goals.

A research study by Gail Matthews, PhD, a clinical psychologist at Dominica University of California, revealed that people with written goals achieve 50% more of their goals than those who don't set clear objectives. You can read more about her study here:

www.bit.ly/Goals-Study

3. Create a 3-hour block

For most people, to reach a goal of 2,000 words per day, it takes about three hours each day. For some people it may take slightly more or slightly less time per day. This really depends on your mastery of the topic.

This works out to writing about 670 words per hour. If that sounds like a lot to you, don't worry. We'll discuss later some techniques that can help you to write faster and increase your daily word count without having to spend more time writing.

The important thing for right now is that you commit to setting aside three hours of uninterrupted time each day to work on your book. You may be thinking, "But what if I have a full-time job? Where can I find the time to spend three hours on writing each day?"

This is a valid concern. It's an excuse I once used myself. I have a very busy full-time job as the Chief Commercial Officer for a multimillion-dollar company in Tanzania (I don't say this to impress you, but to impress upon you that you can still have a thriving career as a Kindle author without sacrificing your day job). In addition, I maintain a career as a public speaking coach and do a lot of individual coaching online over Skype. Therefore, I really can relate to the concern about not being able to find the time to write.

But for me, saying I'm "too busy to write" was simply an excuse to avoid the task of writing. So what did I do? I blocked out distractions using the following techniques.

RescueTime

First, I set up an application on my laptop called RescueTime (www.RescueTime.com). Running this app gives you access to reports that show where you spend your time. It shares with you how much time you spend on specific websites and applications.

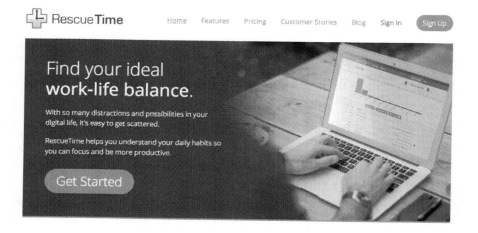

Using RescueTime made me realize just how much time I was wasting online every single day! I was wasting up to four hours online without even realizing it. We've all done it. You get online to check your email quickly and then spend hours on Facebook or other types of surfing.

Blocking the Internet

Once I saw how much wasted time I was spending online, I installed an app that actually blocked me from the Internet. There are many different apps, but my personal favorite is StayFocused (www.bit.ly/Focus-App).

Different apps have different features, but some completely block all sites for a set amount of time or just specific sites such as Facebook or other time-wasting social media sites.

Once I blocked myself from the Internet, I was able to free up a lot more time. I was also less distracted by Facebook and Gmail notifications when I was working. I was able to concentrate all of my efforts on writing and that led to more productivity.

4. The Pomodoro Technique

The Pomodoro Technique is my favorite for writing. It's very simple: You set aside 25 minutes of uninterrupted time to write.

To do this you need to make sure you're in a private, distraction-free environment so that you can give you undivided attention to writing.

The 25-minute block is called a "Pomodoro." You can use a countdown timer to keep track of time – most of us have them on our computers or smartphones. You can also download the free Pomodoro app for your Android phone from Google Play (www.bit.ly/Pomodoro-App) or the $1.99 App for your iPhone from the iTunes store (www.bit.ly/Pomodoro-Apple).

After writing for 25 minutes straight you'll take a five-minute break. Then you'll go back to the next Pomodoro. At the end of four Pomodoros, you'll take a longer break. This one should be at least 15 minutes.

Using this technique for three hours can help you to meet your 2,400-word goal each day. If you meet your goal before the three-hour window, you can then decide whether you want to keep going or call it a day. I prefer to just keep going until I finish my three-hour block so I can complete the book as quickly as possible.

5. Utilize your outline

One thing that will really help you to write faster is that you've already created an outline while you researched. Now all you have to do is follow the structure of your outline as you write.

This can help you to quickly and concisely get across the relevant points. And, of course, as you write it's good to share personal stories and examples to add some depth and personality.

While you write you may find that some items need to be shifted in order, added, or left out. That's okay – your outline is a living document. It's meant to help you, but it shouldn't be so rigid that you don't make any changes.

6. Stream of consciousness writing

This is probably the single best writing tip I've ever received: to use stream of consciousness writing.

What is stream of consciousness writing? It's when you simply write whatever comes to mind without thinking about it too much. Your goal is just to allow your mind to flow with words and to dump as much information as possible on the page.

This isn't a time to worry about quality or editing. You just want to keep writing – in fact your fingers may struggle to keep up with the speed of your thoughts. Just keep writing and writing and let your fingers move quickly across the keyboard.

I say keyboard because most modern writers use laptops, but you can also write your book with traditional pen and paper. Either way, stream of consciousness writing can help you to write a huge number of words in an hour. You may easily be able to write over 1,000 words in one single hour. That makes your goal of 670 words per hour seem pretty doable.

For most writers, the trouble with writing quickly comes from combining the editing and writing phase together. You may find that you want to revise sentences, change paragraphs, and rewrite. But this isn't the time to do that.

With non-fiction writing, you're not trying to win any literature awards. It's more important that your book be concise and clear-cut than that it's poetic. Your writing needs to be in a conversational style as if you're sitting at a table talking with the reader.

The editing phase comes after you've written the book. Don't waste time trying to make your writing perfect. You can allow your writing to be sucky, imperfect, and filled with mistakes. Just write!

Using this technique you should be able to easily write more than 2,000 words a day and in six days you'll have your first draft done. It won't read great, but it will be done. Remember, for now that's your only goal.

Days 6 – 12: Writing Task

For this block of time you want to dedicate each day to actually write the copy for your book. Make sure to:

- Estimate the length of your book
- Set a goal for words to write each day
- Choose the best techniques for helping you to become free from distractions and write as fast as possible

Once you have a first draft, you can move on to the next step of editing your book.

Chapter Eight

HOW TO POLISH YOUR FIRST DRAFT AND MAKE IT SHINE

~

DAYS 6 – 12: EDIT YOUR FIRST DRAFT

Now that you've completed your first draft, it's time to refine it so that you have something readable, concise, and that flows well. The editing process allows you to do just that.

There are several things I do in the editing process that will also benefit you as a writer of non-fiction books. This chapter is filled with simple editing tips that make the process easy to understand.

My Best Editing Tips

These are the steps that I follow during the editing process. I find that editing is a lot less painful as I develop a strategy for doing it.

Make structural changes

As I read through my first draft, I'll go ahead and move paragraphs and chapters around until I feel that it reads logically. It's not unusual to feel that the flow of the book needs some help. Each chapter should logically lead to the next and each paragraph should do the same.

Adjust the tone

Generally, you want a non-fiction book to have a conversational tone. You want your readers to feel like they're having a discussion with you. However, sometimes I quote a lot of research studies in my books and that tone is very academic.

I also may slip into the habit of writing in the passive tense rather than in the active tense. For example, I might use passive voice to say, "Six books were written by John," instead of using active voice to say, "John wrote six books."

So, when I'm editing my book I go ahead and review the tone to make it more conversational. I avoid using complicated, large words and try to replace any academic-sounding passages with shorter, more common language.

Cut out irrelevant ideas

After writing several books, I've found that I have a tendency to overexplain myself. Many authors do this. I can end up being repetitive while trying to get my point across. But with non-fiction Kindle books it's best to be concise.

As I go through my book, I cut down any paragraphs that drone on to explain a concept. I want my paragraphs to express the bare essentials. This process usually causes me to toss out at least 10-15% of my book.

Add personality

The most interesting Kindle books have plenty of examples and stories to back up their points. When reading through my own work, I'm on the lookout to see whether I can add more personal examples and stories to make the book more engaging for my readers.

Adding in short personal examples allows your readers to learn from your experiences – both good and bad. And it makes the book more interesting. You'll find that you develop a more loyal following for future books because your readers feel like they know you.

Break up paragraphs

Kindle books should be easy to read and scan. If you have a lot of long paragraphs, it can make reading digital content unpleasant. Therefore, when editing I look for ways to break up long paragraphs into shorter ones.

Correct grammar

Finally, I will correct any grammar or spelling errors in my text. I use Word's spellcheck tool to spot any errors I may have missed. I do my best to fix major errors, but I don't spend too much time fretting about it because I have an editor who will take care of this as well.

Add important content

During the editing process I also add some content to the book. These three additions are important:

"In a Nutshell" (or similarly titled) section: At the end of each chapter I like to add a quick, bulleted summary of the two or three main points in the chapter that helps readers to get the main ideas. You may have noticed that I've done this as you've read this book.

"Wrap Up" section: I add this section to the end of the book to offer up a list of main points I discussed throughout the book. Readers quickly forget information they read, so having a summary is a valuable tool.

To do this, you need to go through the book and start making a list of main points in each chapter that you can put together. This book, for example, contains the chapter called "Wrap Up" which will contain these points.

Title page: All books need to have a title page at the beginning of the book. I like to keep mine very short. Here's the format for my title pages:

Title of book

© Author Name

Author Website

Don't forget to add your title page to give the book a professional look and feel.

Free offer: I also like to give a free offer so that I can begin to build an email list and fan base. This allows me to market directly to my fans when I launch my next book.

I put this offer at the front of the book instead of at the end. Why? Because Amazon allows customers to preview the first 10% of the book. This means I can give potential customers a free offer and they can sign up to my website even if they don't buy the book (see image below as an example).

It may seem counterintuitive to give something away for free, but this is a great way for me to stay in touch with my customers, provide them with value, and eventually make sales as my readers learn to trust me.

"Questions and Comments" section: I include a "Questions and Comments" section near the end of the book so that readers can get in touch with me if they want. I also include information about my coaching services.

This page has been invaluable for me. I've received over 20 coaching requests in the past month as a result of this page. Plus, I ended up with a consulting job with the Government of Dubai because one of the Dubai government members read my book and then decided to contact me (thank you, Jo!).

Including this section makes it easy for people to get in touch with you and give you feedback as well as offer new business opportunities.

This is also the section where I ask readers to leave a review on Amazon if they enjoyed this book. It's always best to ask for reviews – simply asking will increase the chances that the reader takes the time to do it. You can see an example of this at the end of this book.

"You Might Also Like" page: This is a section where I can direct readers to two or three other books I've written that I think they will like. I include the image of the book cover, excerpts of three positive reviews, and a link to the book's page on Amazon. You'll see an example of this at the end of this book.

Repeat the free gift: I also include the same offer that's at the front of the book at the end. Perhaps in the beginning, readers didn't trust me enough to sign up for my newsletter. But now that they've read to the end they're ready to join.

It's also important to note that I make sure my free gift is very valuable and a good resource. I give away items such as eBooks, short tutorials, MP3s, and videos that I could easily charge for.

By giving this information for free, readers see that I provide value and will be more likely to buy my books and other products in the future.

Bonus: Creating a Website and Newsletter

If you don't already have a website and an email newsletter, then you might be struggling to see how this applies to you. Before you publish your book, you need to go ahead and complete the process of creating these tools.

Here's what you need to do:

Set up a website/blog

These days it's easier than ever to set up a website on Wordpress (www.wordpress.com) or Blogger (www.blogger.com). You can check out these tutorials on how to do so here:

http://learn.wordpress.com/get-started/

https://support.google.com/blogger/answer/1623800?hl=en&ref_topic=3339243

Another choice is FlareSpot (www.FlareSpot.com). **Disclosure**: FlareSpot is a website I created to allow authors, entrepreneurs, and information marketers to quickly and easily create beautiful websites and capture new leads. *Note:* At the time of this publication, FlareSpot is not yet available to the public (though, when it is in several months time, it will be free of charge).

I was very frustrated when trying to create my own website and realized that others must be, too. I hired a team to create a product that would allow anyone to quickly create a website – the result is FlareSpot.

Creating a website with FlareSpot is easy. If you can create a Word document or a Facebook page, you can create a website using this program. You don't need to know any coding. You can just create an account and then write your content.

This site also integrates email newsletters and allows you to connect with Mailchimp, Aweber, or any other email delivery system.

Get your own domain name

When you create a blog on Wordpress, Blogger, or FlareSpot it's free to use the free domain name. For example:

www.akash.flarespot.com or www.akash.wordpress.com

While these are free, they aren't very professional. You'll want to purchase your own domain name to create a more professional-looking site. Domain names are usually an inexpensive investment – mine is only $15/year. You can buy the domain name directly from Wordpress, Blogspot, or FlareSpot or you can use a domain name broker such as NameCheap (www.namecheap.com) or GoDaddy (www.godaddy.com).

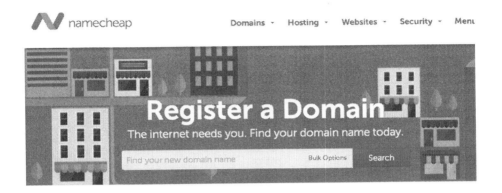

Set up an email newsletter

There are several options for setting up a newsletter, but the two most popular are Aweber (www.aweber.com) and Mailchimp (www.mailchimp.com). I choose to use Mailchimp because they allow you 2,000 free subscribers. If you're just starting out this is a great deal.

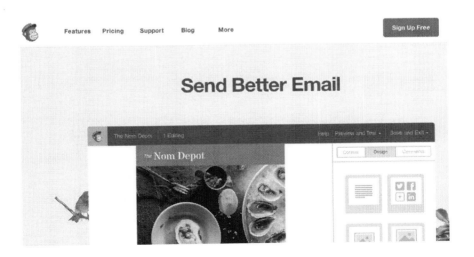

This allows you to get started without having to invest anything at all. Once you set up your newsletter you can integrate it with your website. You can do this by adding a subscription form to your site.

Create something to give away for free

In order to entice your readers to sign up for your list, you'll need to give them something of value. Over the years, I've written eBooks, created videos, and conducted expert interviews that I've used as free gifts.

Do you have some great information that you could give away? If you have several books, you could give away one chapter from each book. You could also write a short report (15-20 pages) on a topic that will interest your readers to give away.

Don't Let Editing Paralyze You

Editing your work is easier said than done. It can be a grueling process to cut out content you've written and make changes. But, this leads to a better experience for your readers and is an important step.

This task is critical, so I spend at least two full days on editing my first draft. You want to spend time on it and be thorough, but it's okay if it's not perfect at this step in this process. Don't fret and fret about each and every imperfection.

Days 6 – 12: Editing Tasks

Once your first draft is complete, you'll want to:

- Make structural changes
- Keep the tone conversational
- Cut out anything irrelevant or repeated
- Add personality
- Add important content such as free gifts, requests for reviews, and other products the reader might like
- Break up big paragraphs
- Create a website and newsletter, if you don't already have them

Once you've completed your own editing session, it's time to get a professional to take a look. You'll learn about that in the next chapter.

Chapter Nine

HIRING A PROFESSIONAL EDITOR – WITHOUT GOING BROKE

~

DAYS 12 – 14: SEND YOUR BOOK TO AN EDITOR

After editing your own book, you might be tempted to upload it straight to Amazon, but I highly advise against this. Why? Because even if you have a great eye for details, you may miss some obvious mistakes since you wrote the book.

Your mind has a tendency to overlook errors that you've made. It's important, then, to send it to a professional editor. This will keep you from getting negative reviews because of silly errors that could have been easily avoided.

The Benefits of Hiring a Professional Editor

Hiring a professional editor can help to insure that your work is free from errors. A professional can carefully examine your book and correct any grammatical or structural errors you've made.

For my own books, my editor plays a crucial role in success. She polishes up the quality of my writing so that I can write faster. Let me explain.

It took me two years to write my first book, *Speak Like a Winner* Why? Because I didn't have an editor. I spent hundreds of hours reading and rereading my book to catch every mistake and make tiny changes.

I was so worried about missing mistakes that I agonized over that book for the better part of a year! Finally, when I did publish my book, readers still found errors I had missed. I ended up having to hire an editor anyway.

With my second book, *How to Deliver a Great Ted Talk*, I was able to crunch out a rough first edit of the book in less than a month (about 40,000 words!). Then, instead of agonizing over mistakes I spent two days making some edits and sent it to my editor.

She spent a couple of days reviewing the book and corrected a lot of my mistakes. Then I sent the book to another editor, just in case my first editor had missed anything. I got an even more improved version back within a couple of days.

Following this procedure, I was able to complete the entire writing, editing and publishing process much quicker than it would have taken otherwise.

It Takes a Team

If you want to make money from your words, you need to see writing as an art as well as a business. To run a business you need to make some investments. It helps to hire smart people who are good at what they do.

My own Kindle team involves a graphic designer, two editors, and a virtual assistant who helps me handle marketing. Each one of these people is worth the investment.

"Akash, what if I don't have enough money to hire an editor? Can't I just ask my friends and family members to help me edit my book?" Unless your friends and family members are professional editors with a strong grasp of the English language, I advise against this.

When I asked my own friends for help with this, I got so many conflicting opinions that it paralyzed me. You can always ask for feedback from friends and family, but it's better to have a professional editor for a professional result.

Hiring an editor doesn't have to be expensive. My editors only charge me $5 for every 250 words (I was able to negotiate such a low rate because I've signed them on for multiple projects). For a 14,000-word manuscript that's a total of only $56. You don't have to hire two editors like I do, but you do need to hire at least one!

You're already investing so much time and energy into your book. Why not spend $50-$100 to get professional editing so that it reads well and gets great reviews? Your investment will pay off in increased sales.

Creating Your Editing Team

Now that you know how important it is to have an editing team, you may be wondering how to hire someone professional to help you. If you haven't already built a team of Kindle editors and designers, you'll need to begin to search for an editor on Day 5.

The best two resources for hiring editors are Elance (www.elance.com) and oDesk (www.odesk.com). Both are good sources and offer competitive rates. Personally I use Elance, but I have many friends who rely on oDesk.

The process for hiring on Elance and oDesk is the same, but I will talk about Elance below to simplify things.

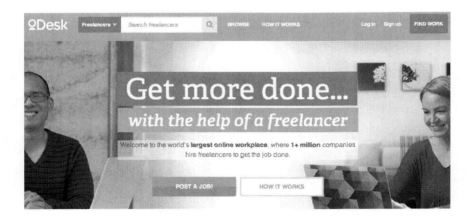

To hire an editor on Elance, you'll log into your Elance account and create a new job. Here's the job template I use:

Edit my 15,000 word eBook

I'm looking for someone to edit my upcoming eBook. The editor needs to have a strong grasp of the English language and a proven track record.

You should be able to correct grammar, punctuation, spelling mistakes and change the sentences to make them flow better.

The eBook is short – less than 15,000 words.

I'm looking for high quality editing at a low, affordable price. Reply with the words "Yellow Umbrella" in your replay so I know you've read this job description.

What's your best price?

I always add the phrase "reply with the words 'Yellow Umbrella' in your reply so that I know you've read the job description." I do this to narrow down freelancers to those who have really read the description.

Some freelancers will bid for your job without really reading the description. You don't want that type of editor for your book.

Once you make your job live, you'll start receiving proposals. You can immediately weed out anyone who doesn't use your code words in his or her reply. You want someone with attention to detail for your editing job.

You will then be left with several freelancers. You'll need to go through each profile and look at reviews. While it may seem unfair to new freelancers, I only work those who have a proven track record.

I look for freelancers who have at least 10 projects under their belt with at least a 95% positive review rating (some bad reviews are expected, especially when a freelancer has a lot of projects under his or her belt). These are my criteria and you're free to choose your own – but this is a good system if you're new to outsourcing.

Now that you've narrowed it down even more, you'll want to test their work with a small project. I select what I think are the top three bids and send them a message saying I'd like to test their services before I give a full project.

For this, I negotiate a rate of about $1 for 250 words and send a 1,000-word document to edit. This ends up being $4 per freelancer. Of course, not everyone accepts this rate, so you do have to negotiate. When I get samples back, I look at the quality and choose the freelancer that I feel did the best job.

I also like to hire a second editor to go through the book after the first editor just to double-check that there aren't any errors.

Avoid Hiring Editors on Fiverr

Fiverr is an excellent resource for some services such as graphic design. But it doesn't seem to provide the same quality when it comes to editors. I've tried several editors from Fiverr but have always been disappointed by their quality.

It seems like a good site to hire someone and save money, but with editing you get what you pay for. Feel free to experiment if you want to see for yourself. However, be sure to always test editors with a shorter piece of text.

Editing Results

After you send your book off to an editor, it may take 2-3 days to get it returned. I have a good working relationship with my editors and get priority treatment. But, this can take time to establish.

When you get your book back, look through it. If you feel that it needs more work, don't be afraid to send it back and ask for more specifics about what you still need.

Days 12 – 14: Editing Tasks

The main tasks you need for this part of your book creation include:

- Hiring an editing team if you don't already have one in place
- Sending your book off to be edited
- Reviewing edits and sending it back again if needed

You'll have a few days in between sending off the book and getting it back. In the next chapter we'll discuss what you can do during this time to stay productive.

But this is a good time to take a moment and give yourself a pat on the back. You've accomplished a great deal by researching, outlining, writing, and editing your book.

Chapter Ten

NINJA TECHNIQUES TO FIND PEOPLE TO REVIEW YOUR BOOKS ON AMAZON

~

DAY 13: ASK FOR REVIEWS

At this point the bulk of your work is done and you have some time to wait for your editor to send back your book. This is a good time to start looking for reviewers. The more reviews you have for your book, the better your sales will be.

Where to Find Reviewers

It can be overwhelming to think of soliciting reviews from people for a book that isn't totally finished. But this is an important part of the process and shouldn't be skipped. I've had success finding reviewers with the techniques outlined below.

Email list

If you've already established your email list, you can send an email to your subscribers and let them know about your new book. You can offer to give out review copies in exchange for a review on Amazon. Here's the email template that I use:

Subject line: Free Review Copy of "Ready, Set –
PROCRASTINATE" book

<< First Name >>, as a subscriber to my list, I would like
to offer you a **free review copy** my newest book, "Ready,
Set – PROCRASTINATE! 23 Anti-Procrastination Tools
Designed to Help You Stop Putting Things Off and Start
Getting Things Done!"

http://eepurl.com/P9kvb

If you want to stop dreaming and start doing, you must
develop the "now" habit. This book will show you how to
do just that. In it, you will learn how to:

• **Tackle any task using the solar-flaring technique.**

• Complete large, complex tasks using the Lego block
technique.

• **Trick yourself into working on any project using the
five-minute technique.**

• Eliminate procrastinator-talk using a simple eight-step
method

• **Instantly increase your motivation using two simple
words.**

•Tackle perfectionist thoughts that cause you to
procrastinate.

• **Beat procrastination using Dan Ariely's simple trick.**

• Make inherently boring tasks more interesting.

• **Create positive new habits using the Seinfeld calendar.**

If you have a valid Amazon account and are willing to review the book on Amazon, then please sign up to receive a free review copy here:

http://eepurl.com/P9kvb

Thanks,

Akash Karia

If you haven't already set up your email list, you should! I can't stress this point enough. Go ahead and set up a blog on Wordpress, Blogger, or FlareSpot. You'll learn more about how to generate traffic to your blog later.

But, even if you don't have an email list, you can use the following "ninja" techniques to find reviewers for your book...

Facebook groups

If you haven't got an existing list, you can join Facebook groups on your niche. For example, I have written a number of books on public speaking. I searched for "public speaking" groups on

Facebook and joined several of them. There are also a lot of author groups on Facebook that you can join and post review requests on. (Of course, be sure to read the group rules before you post.)

Here are some examples:

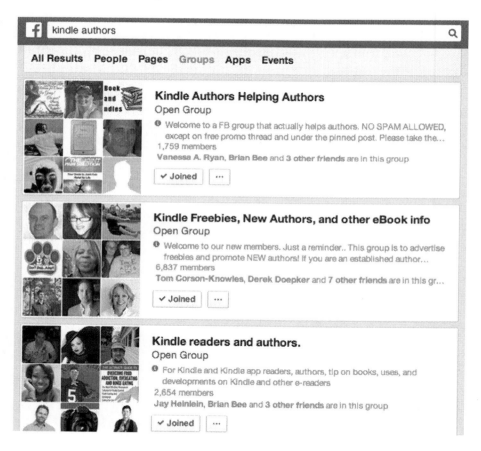

Once I had been approved to join, I posted a message saying that I had a book titled *How to Design TED-Worthy Presentation Slides,* and that if anyone was interested in receiving a free copy in exchange for a review on Amazon, I'd be happy to send one.

I quickly had over 20 people sign up for review copies. I gave out all of those copies as promised.

Not everyone who signs up to review your book will do so. In this example, I had more than 50 people sign up to review the book, but only seven actually did it. However, now I have a good list of seven people to reach out to in the future.

LinkedIn groups

LinkedIn is also a very powerful tool. You can join many professional groups, introduce yourself, and participate in the discussions. This gives you a great place to post offers for free book reviews.

You want to make sure that you're not too promotional on this site because you can get kicked out of a group that doesn't like self-promotion. As a professional speaker and author of books on public speaking, I joined over 30 groups on public speaking. You can see this on my LinkedIn profile:

In addition, I also created by own group titled "Public Speaking and Presentation Skills for Professional Speakers" (www.bit.ly/AkashGroup). I then invited those in my network to join. Once I had over 200 people from my network join the group, I found more and more people kept joining.

Now I have over 8,697 members in my group. (Initially I had to work very hard in sending out messages to members of similar groups, asking them if they would be interested in joining my group too – but now that the group has grown to a sizeable number, it grows by itself.) LinkedIn allows me to send a message to these people once each week – which I do. I always make sure I offer value in the messages I send out.

Usually I use this message to send out free tips on public speaking. But I do also ask for reviews on my books and occasionally promote some of my paid books.

Competitor reviewers

The final technique (and the most "ninja" of them all) for finding reviewers is to browse through your competitors' books.

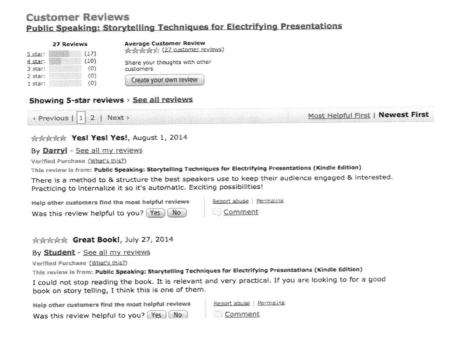

When you click on the names of reviewers, you'll be led to an Amazon review page.

You'll be able to see all the reviews that person has posted. You can check to see whether they are generally positive and constructive rather than harsh and negative. In some cases, the reviewer's email is also on this page.

If you like their reviews, you can write a short email explaining that you came across their review and since they enjoyed your competitor's book, would they be interested in reviewing yours?

Sometimes you can't see the reviewer's email address, but there is a website you can use to contact them. This step does take a lot of time and work, but you can also skip the work by hiring a virtual assistant.

There are many great virtual assistants on Fiverr who are willing to do two or three hours of work for just $5.

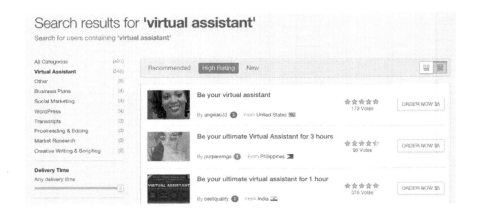

Hiring a virtual assistant will allow you to get the research that you need without having to spend a lot of time doing it.

What Next?

Once you find people who are willing to review your book, you need to send them a copy of the finalized version. I usually send out PDF copies. But you'll also need to follow up to remind the readers to review the book.

Many people forget to write the review or even read the book. Some people will never actually write the review, but many people will with a little bit of pressure from reminder emails.

It's good to send out reminders within two weeks, one month, and two months of emailing out the finalized book. You don't need to be aggressive. This email should be a friendly reminder to check on their progress with the book. For example, here's the reminder email I sent to reviewers one month after they'd signed up to receive my book (feel free to steal this or any of the other email templates I share in this book for your own use):

Subject: Hi *|FNAME|*, did you get your book? + review request

> << First Name >>, I hope you've received your free review copy of "Anti-Procrastination: 23 Tools to Stop Procrastinating and Get Stuff Done".
>
> You'd applied for a free review copy about a month ago through my website
>
> Anyway, this is a quick request: If you enjoyed the book, please leave a review on Amazon.
>
> www.bit.ly/AntiProcrastination
>
> By the way, the book is currently FREE on Amazon today so that you can download a copy to your Kindle before you leave your review:
>
> www.bit.ly/AntiProcrastination

Thanks in advance for your review!

Akash Karia

PS - Every review counts! If you found anything of value in the book, then please leave a review! Otherwise, burn the book and don't tell anyone about it ;)

www.bit.ly/AntiProcrastination

If after the third or fourth email they don't reply to you or post a review, you can let it go and find more reviewers.

You need to make sure you have a minimum of six reviews to convince people that your book is worth their time. The more reviews you can get, though, the better!

Day 13: Review Tasks

The more reviews you have of your book, the more purchases you'll have. The reviews you solicit are a good investment. Today, work on finding reviewers for your book so that when it goes live you'll have reviews quickly.

Remember to:

- Send offers for review copies of your book to your email list (or start one if you don't have one yet!)
- Offer review copies on Facebook and LinkedIn groups
- Contact people who have reviewed competitor books
- Send review copies to those who have expressed interest
- Plan to provide friendly reminders to reviewers at two weeks, one month, and two months

This process will help you to have at least the minimum six reviews you need for readers to trust you – and can solicit many more.

Chapter Eleven

FORMATTING YOUR BOOK TO PROVIDE A GREAT READER EXPERIENCE

~

DAY 15: BOOK FORMATTING

Once you have your eBook back from your editors, it's time to format your book to upload it. You can publish to many different sites including:

- Amazon (www.amazon.com)

- Barnes and Noble (www.nookpress.com)

- GooglePlay (www.play.google.com/books)

- Smashwords (www.smashwords.com)

While you'll find that there are even more options, these four tend to garner the greatest traffic and sales. Of those that are listed above, Amazon is by far the biggest. Generally self-published authors earn 80-90% of their income from Amazon and only 10-20% from the other sites combined.

I only publish on Amazon because they are the biggest seller. Plus, by publishing exclusively with them I get some perks.

Should You Use KDP Select?

By enrolling in Amazon exclusively and joining the KDP Select program (www.kdp.amazon.com/select), you'll be able to use their full suite of promotional tools. Ultimately this can help you to sell more books.

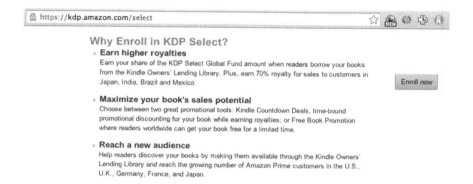

Here's Amazon's explanation of their KDP Select program:

> "When you choose to enroll your book in KDP Select, you're committing to make the digital format of that book available exclusively through KDP. During the period of exclusivity, you cannot distribute your book digitally anywhere else, including on your website, blogs, etc. However, you can continue to distribute your book in physical format, or in any format other than digital." - KDP

Why would you want to make the commitment to Amazon? Because doing so gives you the ability to use two promotional tools: Kindle Countdown Deals and Free Book Promotions. Here's how Amazon describes these:

> "Choose between two great promotional tools: Kindle Countdown Deals, time-bound promotional discounting for your book while earning royalties; or Free Book Promotion where readers worldwide can get your book free for a limited time."

I prefer to utilize these tools because they help me sell a lot more books than I would otherwise (you'll see just how later on in the book).

Free promotions

For example, when I first publish my book I use Amazon's free book promotion and make my book free for five days. I then tell my email list about the free promotion and share it on my social media pages.

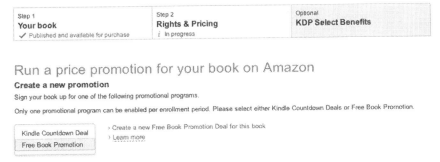

My goal is to get at least 1,000 free book downloads, but some of my promotions have resulted in as many as 40,000 free downloads. If I'm doing this to earn money, why do I offer the book for free? There are a couple of reasons for this.

First, when the book comes off the "free" section and into the "paid" section, it will get a boost in rankings. You'll end up higher on the bestseller lists than you would without the program. Ultimately your higher placement will result in even more sales.

Your book will also begin to appear on other "Customers also bought" listings under competitor books. This is like getting free advertising directly to your niche customers.

By giving away books you can also increase your basic customer base. When I had 40,000 people download my book for free I also added 1,000 names to my email list. This list is made up of my most loyal customers and is a great source of revenue.

And, by giving away books you'll also be able to earn more reviews. This also helps increase your sales as people read the reviews. As you begin to have more reviews, you'll see that some of them can be negative.

Don't let negative reviews worry you as long as you have many positive reviews as well. Of course if you have a lot of negative reviews you need to look at the quality of your book again.

After the free promotion, my book usually ends up selling between three and five copies per day. When I have launched books without the free promotion, the sales have struggled with less than one copy per day.

As another example of the power of Amazon's free promotion, check out the results from Michal Stawicki's free promo for one of his books (via FireYourMentor):

"My sales before the promo were just below 1 sale per day threshold.

The promo was 5 days long (30X-3.XI.2013). I bought a gig on Fiverr to spread the word. 30 freebies pages, several Twitts and 5 FB messages. It didn't work very well for me. But my time spend on uploading the info about the promo to the freebies sites would cost a similar amount ($35). So I don't consider this money totally wasted.

I also posted in about a dozen freebies groups on FB (about 30k members put together). My ugly, Fiverr-made cover was used for the promo.

I'm sure it affected the number of free downloads. After the promo I was provided with the better cover and immediately changed it, so actual sales were done with the new one.

The results: 871 downloads at amazon.com, 76 on different markets and surprise, surprise – 144 on amazon.co.jp. It went "viral" there, I guess.

The first 2 days after the promo I sold 4 my other books and not even 1 of the book which has been promoted. Well, I sold 2 on co.jp.

days 3-4: 5 more books sold and 3 more on co.jp

day 5: 7 books sold! My record

day 6: 6 books sold

day 7: 3 books sold

day 8: 2 books sold

day 9: 1 books sold

day 10: 4 books sold

day 11: 15 books sold! Another daily record

day 12: 4 books sold

day 13: 4 books sold

day 14: 3 books sold

day 15: 5 books sold

day 16: 1 book sold

I also sold 30 more books on co.jp (almost exclusively the promoted title) and about 10 more on different international markets.

In the middle of November I did another promo. The results: 939 downloads at amazon.com, 70 on different markets. Now my sales are about 5 books a day." - www.expandbeyondyourself.com

The KDP free promos have worked for me, and as you can see, they've worked for Michal too! Try the free promos out – they might work for you too...

KDP Countdown Deals

The KDP Countdown deals can also help your book to have more success. Three months after the free promotion, I use the KDP Countdown deals to discount books. This tool allows you to lower the price of any book that's regularly listed over $2.99 to anything as low as $0.99. The reason it's called a "Countdown" deal is because during your book's promotion, readers can see a countdown timer showing how long the deal is valid (see image below):

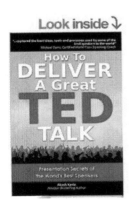

Before I discounted the book, it was selling approximately four copies per day. During the discount promotion, the book sales shot up to more than 100 copies each day. This helped to push me further up the bestseller lists. In fact, during the countdown promo, the book broke into the Amazon Top 200 books overall and pushed my author rank up to #11 in the Business & Investing category (needless to say, I was absolutely thrilled!).

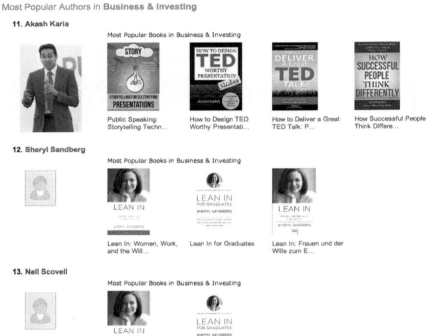

Amazon also promotes discounted books and because there's a time limit to the promotion, you have a higher conversion rate of browsers into buyers for your book. Once the book's discounted promotion ended, sales naturally declined and have now settled at 13-15 per day. But as you can see, that's almost four times as many as I was selling initially.

When to Choose KDP Select

While I don't recommend that everyone sign up for KDP Select, I do recommend it for any author who doesn't have an established fan base. The free promotions and countdown programs can help you to build that following you need.

If you already have a large email list, you may want to skip the Amazon exclusivity and make your book available on many different platforms. With your own large customer base, you may not need the access to Amazon's tools, though anyone can benefit from them.

How to Format Your Book

Now let's go to the more technical information of actually formatting your book for publishing. Amazon and other retailers state that you can upload your book in Word or PDF format – but when you do that the conversion quality to the final book is terrible.

Instead, you want to upload your book to all the retailers as an ePub file. Amazon, Barnes and Noble, Smashwords, and Google Play all work well with ePub files.

Converting to ePub

While you can convert your book yourself to an ePub file, I find that it's a time-consuming process. If you're dead set on doing it yourself, you might want to check out a tool called Calibre (www.calibre-ebook.com). This is a free tool I've used before to convert Word documents to ePub files.

However, I find that I'd rather outsource this formatting to someone else. It may cost a little money, but it frees me up to do things that are more valuable with my time and actually saves me money in the end.

You can find great freelancers on Elance and on Fiverr to help you with the conversion. If you're not sure what to ask, it can help to have a template to guide you. The following is the exact template I used when I was looking to hire the person who did my book conversion:

> "I've got a 125 page Word-document that needs to be formatted for Kindle.
>
> Nothing major required.
>
> I have no pictures or tables.
>
> Mostly text, a couple of hyperlinks.

I'll send you the Word file and you can format it for Kindle (MOBI version required).

I'm anticipating this will be an easy job for someone who's already done it before.

What's your best price? :-)

Oh, and while we're at it, how much for formatting it as an ePUB too?

When responding to this job, please provide samples of previous books you've formatted and reply with the word 'pink elephant' so I know that you've read this job description.

Thanks,

Akash

P.S. I have three more eBooks that need formatting, so if I'm happy with the first one, I'll come back to you again for the other three."

You can use this template and replace it with your own specific information.

You can also use several websites that specialize in turning your Word document to ePub and MOBI files, but (in my opinion) these can actually be very expensive.

Seeing how ridiculously expensive some of these can be, I teamed up with several reliable freelancers to set up my own conversion team. My team currently handles the conversion of books that are 20,000 words or fewer for $60.

For books that are less than 40,000 words, the cost is less than $120. Check out the pricing here: www.AkashKaria.com/BookFormatting

(**Full disclosure**: While I am recommending my company because I think our rates are very competitive, you should still browse on Elance and Fiverr for eBook conversion specialists).

Once you've hired a freelancer to convert your book to ePub, you can send him or her the Word document and then wait. It shouldn't take long to get your book back and you're almost done!

Day 14: Formatting Task

Today you'll need to get to work on preparing your book to be published. In a nutshell, I recommend:

- Choosing the sites that you'll publish to (I recommend Amazon KDP Select if you're just starting out).
- Formatting your book to ePub using outsourcing if possible.

And once those things are done, it's time to actually publish your book. You'll learn my secrets to promoting your book as well in the next chapter.

Chapter Twelve (Bonus)

PUBLISH – HOW TO MAKE A SPLASH AND GET MAXIMUM VISIBILITY FOR YOUR BOOK

~

DAY 16: PUBLISH

Note: I know that this book's title promises you "How to Write a Non-Fiction Kindle eBook in 15 Days" but you'll notice that I've added in one more bonus day – day 16 that walks you through the process of actually publishing your work; The reason I've done this is because I had a lot of readers contacting me asking me to help them with the technicalities of publishing their book online, so I decided to add in this new bonus chapter as a way of going the extra mile for you.

~

Now that you have the book back from your formatter, it's time to publish it! This is the final step of becoming a published author and is really quite simple if you have a solid plan. In this chapter you'll learn the best way to release your book for maximum sales.

First you'll need to choose the sites where you wish to publish such as Amazon, Barnes & Noble, or GooglePlay. Then you'll go ahead and upload the MOBI or the ePub format to the site. Each one of these sites has a slightly different procedure, but overall you'll upload your cover as one file and then upload the file as another.

Publishing on Amazon

1 – Create and **sign into your Amazon Kindle Direct Publishing account** at www.amazonkdp.com

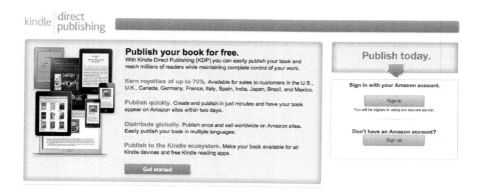

2 – **Select "Add New Title"**

3 – **Enroll in the "KDP Select" program if you'd like to utilize Amazon's promotional tools** such as the Free Promotions and the Countdown Deals. Note that this means you must make your book exclusive to Amazon and cannot sell the digital version anywhere else on the web, including your own website.

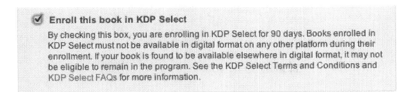

4 – **Fill out all the necessary information**, such as the book title and book description (make sure to write a compelling, benefit-driven book description that shows your potential readers the massive value they'll receive by reading your book).

5 – **Choose two appropriate categories for your book**. Categories are Amazon's virtual bookshelves and you can decide which two bookshelves you want your book displayed on. Obviously, you want to choose categories that are related to your book's topic, but you also want to choose categories where your book will be ranked well.

Choose categories (up to two):

Filter | All | Fiction | Nonfiction

⊞ ARCHITECTURE
⊞ ART
⊞ BIBLES
⊞ BIOGRAPHY & AUTOBIOGRAPHY
⊞ BODY, MIND & SPIRIT
⊟ BUSINESS & ECONOMICS
  ☐ General
  ⊞ Accounting
  ☐ Advertising & Promotion
  ☐ Auditing

Selected categories:

Choose a category

For example, I currently have a book titled *Anti Negativity* (bit.ly/AntiNegativityUS). It was very tempting to place the book under the following category without doing much research:

Kindle Store > Kindle eBooks > Nonfiction > Self-Help > Happiness

However, when I explore books in this category, I see that this is a very competitive category! At the time of this writing, the number one best-selling book in the category has an amazing sales rank of #653; the 10th best-selling book has an impressive sales rank of #5,780; the 20th best-selling book has an equally impressive sales rank of #9,579.

To me, this is a very tough category to rank in the Top 20 for, and if you don't rank in the Top 20, it's harder for readers to discover your book when browsing that category. Therefore, it's best to find another category where there's enough demand for the books but where it's easier to rank in the Top 20.

After exploring on Amazon for some time and paying attention to the categories of my competitors' books, I come across the following category:

Kindle Store > Kindle eBooks > Health, Fitness & Dieting > Psychology & Counseling > Experimental Psychology

I can see that this category is much less competitive. While the top five books in the bestseller rankings have a sales rank of less than 10,000, the next five books have a ranking in the mid 20,000's. This tells me that there is still demand in that category (i.e. there are enough readers browsing the category to give the top 10 books a decent number of sales), but it's not overly competitive (meaning that it'll be easier for my book to rank in the Top 20 and thus profit from being high on the bestseller lists).

In fact, having placed my book under this category, it now sits at the #6 spot and enjoys a decent number of sales every day.

To conclude, I'll say that choosing the right categories is not an easy task. It's more of an art than a science. You'll need to explore competitors' books and try to find a category with enough demand but one where it's not impossible to rank in the top 20. Experiment around with different categories and don't be afraid to change categories – your choice doesn't have to be permanent!

6 – Upload the book cover and the MOBI/ePUB file

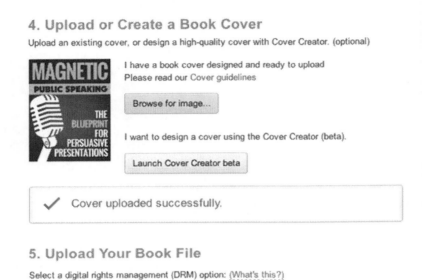

4. Upload or Create a Book Cover

Upload an existing cover, or design a high-quality cover with Cover Creator. (optional)

I have a book cover designed and ready to upload
Please read our Cover guidelines

Browse for image...

I want to design a cover using the Cover Creator (beta).

Launch Cover Creator beta

✓ Cover uploaded successfully.

5. Upload Your Book File

Select a digital rights management (DRM) option: (What's this?)

○ Enable digital rights management
◉ Do not enable digital rights management

7 – Verify your publishing territories and set your price

Amazon gives you the option of making your book available worldwide (the option I always choose) or selecting individual countries.

After doing this, you need to decide on the price. If you price your book less than $2.99 or higher than $9.99, you will earn a 35% royalty on your book. Books priced between $2.99 and $9.99 earn a 70% royalty on book sales. We'll talk more about how to price your books within the next couple of pages.

8. Choose Your Royalty

Please select a royalty option for your book. (What's this?)

○ 35% Royalty
◉ 70% Royalty

	List Price	Royalty Rate	Delivery Costs	Estimated Royalty
Amazon.com	$ [2] USD ! Price must be between $2.99 and $9.99.	35% (Why?) 70%		

8 – **Preview your book**. After you've uploaded your book you'll want to test to make sure everything looks good. For example, Amazon allows you to look at a preview. Since you've formatted your book as an ePub/MOBI file, it should go smoothly.

9 – **Publish**. After that you just need to hit publish. On Amazon, your Kindle book should normally be live and ready to be purchased within 24 hours!

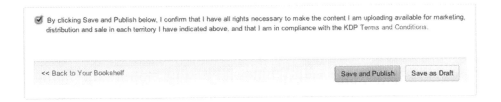

☑ By clicking Save and Publish below, I confirm that I have all rights necessary to make the content I am uploading available for marketing, distribution and sale in each territory I have indicated above, and that I am in compliance with the KDP Terms and Conditions.

<< Back to Your Bookshelf   [Save and Publish] [Save as Draft]

Promoting Your Book

Publishing your book is a great start, but you can't expect people to immediately start buying. You'll need to do more work in the beginning to promote your book and generate sales before the retailers, such as Amazon, start promoting it.

If you already have your own following on social media and a blog, then you might have decided to forgo Amazon's exclusive KDP Select program. In this case, you'll have to do heavy promotion of your own.

You'll need to send out email to your subscribers and share messages about your book on social media. Once a substantial number of people buy your book, it will begin to move up the bestseller charts at each retailer.

The higher up on the bestseller charts the book is, the more visibility it will have. This will lead to increased sales.

KDP Select

If you don't already have a large existing fan base, I recommend that you go ahead and sign up for KDP Select with Amazon. This program will help your book to get traction and reach more people.

You may worry about not having income from other retailers, but for the majority of authors Amazon provides most of the income and their promotional tools help you to reach a greater audience.

I recommend that you set your initial price at $0.99. On Amazon this is the lowest possible price point. You may be wondering why you'd want to make your book so inexpensive. But there's a method to this madness.

At such a low price point, customers will be more tempted to buy your work even if they don't know you. Most people are willing to risk one dollar to find out what you have to say. You're more likely to get impulse buys at this price.

The more sales you have, the higher you'll move up the bestseller list and the more sales you'll have. Sure, at such a low price point and only a 35% royalty rate, you won't be making money, but I recommend launching at this price point until you hit the top 10 in your category (at which point you can increase the price to $2.99+).

Social media

Once you've signed up with KDP Select, you'll still need to promote your book on social media such as Facebook, Twitter, and LinkedIn pages. Ask your friends or fans to share your book as well.

Reviews

You've already asked some people to write reviews. Now that the book is live, it's time to remind them that you'd love to get their review. Provide them with a link to the book on Amazon to make it easy for them.

Free promotion

After you have a couple of reviews, select some free promotion dates. These work best if you have some reviews — six or more is the best. But if you only have a couple that's okay in the beginning.

Schedule the free promotion at least a week ahead of time so that you can notify the sites that promote free eBooks. This will help spread the word about your book, increase your downloads, and help promote your book even more.

Note: If you haven't already, then sign up for *Author Marketing Club* (www.authormarketingclub.com), which provides you with a free book submission tool to submit your book to the top free book promo sites (www.authormarketingclub.com/members/submit-your-book).

Of course, you don't have to necessarily submit to the free book promo sites yourself. You can save time and hire people on Fiverr to do this.

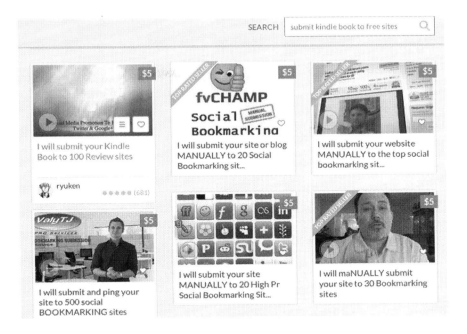

Hiring someone to do this will give you more time to work on writing other books or doing something else that adds value to your business.

Press releases

You can also submit press releases about your book. A press release can allow news sites to pick up the story about your book and promote it for free. Here is a press release I wrote for one of my books.

> Akash Karia, #1 best-selling author of *How to Deliver a Great TED Talk* (www.bit.ly/GreatTED), releases another hot new book titled *Captivate: Public Speaking Secrets from TED Talks* (www.bit.ly/Captivate-TED). The Amazon Kindle book will be free on February 2-6, 2014.

In case you don't know, TED is a global conference whose slogan is "ideas worth spreading." Founded in 1984, TED has become immensely popular. Speakers at the TED conferences include the likes of Bill Gates, Sir Ken Robinson, Dan Pink, Tony Robbins, and Sheryl Sandberg. These talks are available for free viewing on the TED website, and as of 2014 the website boasts an impressive library of over 1,500 talks that have been viewed more than a billion times.

Not only is the content of the TED talks inspiring and thought provoking, the speakers themselves are powerful, persuasive, and engaging.

Presentation expert Akash Karia believes that anyone can learn to deliver powerful TED-like presentations. "I studied over 200 of the best TED talks and analyzed each one line by line to figure out what makes a TED talk sticky. While there is no set formula for delivering a great TED talk, I have discovered that there are certain techniques and tools used by TED speakers that can be used by anyone to spice up their presentations!"

Based on the success of his book, *How to Deliver a Great TED Talk*, which became a #1 bestseller in the public-speaking category on Amazon, Akash launched a new book titled *CAPTIVATE: Public Speaking Secrets from TED Talks*. On February 2-6, Akash is offering the hot new book for free on Amazon: www.bit.ly/Captivate-TED. Readers can download the free book from Amazon on the specified dates to read on their Kindle devices, smartphones and computers.

If you're going to be delivering a TED talk, a TEDx talk or any other speech or presentation, *CAPTIVATE: Public Speaking Secrets from TED Talks* will give you the roadmap for keeping your audiences captivated!

About Akash Karia Consulting

Akash Karia Consulting is a training firm located in Tanzania. Founded by Akash Karia, the firm has trained thousands of people worldwide, from bankers in Hong Kong to yoga teachers in Thailand to senior executives in Dubai. Akash Karia is the author of eight #1 bestsellers on Amazon and writes simple, easy-to-read, step-by-step guides that help people unleash excellence. To download Akash's free eBooks on public speaking, persuasion, and productivity, visit www.AkashKaria.com

Although I wrote the press release myself (yes, I know it feels weird writing about yourself in the third person), I didn't promote it myself. I hired someone on Fiverr to do it for me (just search for "Press Release Submission" on Fiverr). Again, this was a minimal cost and gave me back my time to work on other things. (By the way, feel free to "steal" my PR statement and adapt it to your own book!)

Pricing

I usually keep my books at $0.99 for at least two months in order to maximize sales. Although I don't earn much revenue from this initially, it does maximize sales and help my book to get more visibility.

In the third month, I raise the price to $2.99. The momentum from the free book promotion and the $0.99 price carry on and the book continues selling well at $2.99. I sell most of my books for this price.

However, some of my better-selling and longer books have prices set between $3.99 and $5.99. I continue to monitor my monthly sales against the price point to ensure that I'm maximizing the sales and revenue from each book.

In the fourth month, I use the KDP Select "discounted promotion" and discount my book to $0.99. I promote this discount to my email list and all of my social media pages. Amazon also promotes all discounted promotions.

This combination allows my book to shoot up to the bestseller ranks during the discounted promotions. After the book comes off the promotion, it usually continues to sell well due to an increase in visibility.

After a promotion, a book will generally sell a couple more copies each day than it did before the countdown deal. I continue using this promotion every three months to add new sales and life to my books.

Starting Strong

While my promotion strategy isn't the only way to do things, and I do complement it with guest blogging and email newsletter promotions, I have found that it's a great way to kick off your book sales.

Amazon provides great tools for promoting your book, and the other retailers don't have as many promotion tools. It's harder to get any sales with sites other than Amazon unless you already have a pre-existing database of fans.

That's why I recommend that you start strong using Amazon if you're still building your list. As you sell more books and point your readers to sign up for your newsletter, you'll actually begin to build a solid database of fans who are interested in purchasing from you in the future.

Day 16: Publishing Tasks

Now that you've completed your book, it's time to publish it. Let's review what you need to do on Day 16 to publish and promote your book.

- Upload your book to the appropriate retailer. Again, I recommend Amazon KDP Select.
- Promote your book by emailing to your list, promoting on social media pages, gathering reviews, offering free promotions, and submitting press releases (you can outsource some of these tasks through Fiverr).
- Plan to continue to breathe new life into your book sales by using KDP Select discounted promotions every three months.

And now you've done it! You were able to write a Kindle book in 15 days and have it published by day 16 following this simple, straightforward process. Now it's time to start working on your next book!

Chapter Thirteen

WRAP UP

~

Congratulations!

If you've implemented the techniques and the publishing blueprint covered in this book, you're on your way to publishing your own bestseller!

We've covered a lot of tools and techniques in this short book, so this chapter will serve as a useful summary of the most important principles covered:

NICHE SELECTION

1 – Choose a niche that interests you.

2 – Ensure there is enough demand for your niche.

3 – Narrow down your niche so that your book is focused on just one problem or challenge you can solve.

RESEARCH

4 – Spend at least three full days on research.

5 – Don't wait till you start writing to do your research.

6 – Gather your research from a variety of sources, including Google keywords, blog posts, podcasts, and popular Kindle highlights of competitors' books.

7 – Keep track of all the sources and websites you use for research because you might have to refer back to them and give them credit in your book.

OUTLINE

8 – Outline your book while you research.

9 – Create a rough table of contents.

TITLE

10 – Make sure you know your audience. What problems are they searching for? What benefit can you give them?

11 – Keeping your audience in mind, brainstorm as many titles as you can.

12 – Invite your friends to help you by holding a title party.

13 – Keep your title short and ensure that it clearly conveys the benefit of your book to readers.

14 – Aim for a benefit-driven title such as *How to Win Friends and Influence People* or a curiosity-driven title such as *Becoming the 1%.*

15 – If you opt for a curiosity-driven title, ensure that the subtitle clearly communicates the benefit of the book, e.g., *Becoming the 1%: How to Master Time Management and Rise to the Top in 7 Days.*

16 – Try to include your topic keyword in your title to help readers discover your book when they search for that topic on Amazon.

17 – Test your title using Facebook and Twitter votes, ad variations, and email subject line A/B testing.

18 – Through a process of elimination, narrow your titles down to no more than two.

19 – Commit to a working title and remember that your choice doesn't have to be permanent!

COVER

20 – Hire a cover designer on Fiverr, Elance, or 99Designs (depending on your budget).

21 – Clearly explain to your designer what your book is about.

22 – Provide your designer with samples of covers you like and explain why you like them.

23 – Stress the importance of having a large, readable title that is visible even when the cover is reduced to a thumbnail on Amazon.

24 – Aim for a simple cover with high contrast between the image/background and the text.

25 – Don't be afraid to ask your designer for revisions until you're happy.

26 – Test your cover by posting the covers on Facebook and asking for votes.

27 – Test the cover using Facebook (or LinkedIn) ad variations, changing only the image between the ads and monitoring the click-through rates.

28 – If your book sales are lagging, try uploading a new cover and see how this impacts sales.

WRITE THE FIRST DRAFT – FAST!

29 – Estimate your book length. Most Kindle books are 12,000 to 30,000 words long.

39 – Set a daily word count goal so that you can finish writing the book within the required number of days.

40 – Write down your word-count goal and stick it somewhere you can see it because research shows that people with written

goals achieve 50% more of their goals than those who don't set any clear objectives.

41 – Set aside a block of time where you can work uninterrupted on your writing.

42 – Use the RescueTime app to discover what online activities are wasting most of your time and eliminate those from your life so that you have more time to write.

43 – Eliminate distractions on the internet using the StayFocused app.

44 – Utilize the Pomodoro Technique to make the writing process more efficient.

45 – Write using your outline.

46 – Use stream of consciousness writing. Allow the words to flow from you onto the paper without trying to edit what you're writing.

EDIT YOUR FIRST DRAFT

47 – Carefully go through your first draft and make structural changes to paragraphs as well as chapters to ensure that your book reads smoothly and logically.

48 – Adjust the tone (if necessary) so that your language is simple and conversational.

49 – Be on the lookout for any irrelevant or repetitive ideas that you can cut out.

50 – Add personality to your book by adding personal stories and examples wherever you can.

51 – Break up long paragraphs into shorter ones so that your book is easier to read on eBook devices.

52 – Correct the grammar and spelling errors in your text.

53 – Add in important front and back matter to your book to give it a more professional look and feel.

BUILD YOUR EMAIL LIST

54 – Set up your blog or website using Wordpress, Blogger, or FlareSpot.

55 – Register your domain name via NameCheap or GoDaddy.

56 – Set up your mailing list using Aweber or Mailchimp.

57 – Create a lead magnet (a free ebook, MP3, or video) that you can give away for free to your website readers in exchange for their email address.

HIRE A PRO TO EDIT YOUR WORK

58 – Hire a professional editor on Elance or oDesk to carefully scrutinize and correct your work. Elance and oDesk are great places to find freelance editors.

59 – Avoid hiring editors on Fiverr.

60 – Work with editors who have a proven track record with at least 10 projects under their belt and at least a 95% positive review rating.

61 – Select three editors who seem like a good fit and test their skills by hiring them to edit only a small portion of your book (250-500 words).

62 – Select the editor who gives you back the best-edited sample to work on your full project.

63 – Don't settle! Don't be afraid to ask the editor for a double-check if you're not fully satisfied with the work.

ASK FOR ADVANCE REVIEWS

64 – Send offers for review copies of your book to your email list (you have already started one, haven't you?).

65 – Offer review copies on Facebook and LinkedIn groups.

66 – Contact people who have reviewed competitor books.

67 – Send review copies to those who have expressed interest.

68 – Provide friendly reminders to reviewers at two weeks, one month, and two months.

FORMAT YOUR BOOK

69 – Choose the sites that you'll publish to (I recommend Amazon KDP Select if you're just starting out).

70 – Outsource the formatting of your book to ePub or MOBI on Fiverr, Elance or oDesk.

PUBLISH YOUR BOOK

71 – Upload your final ePub/MOBI file and the cover art to the desired platforms (Amazon, Barnes & Noble, GooglePlay, Smashwords, etc.).

72 – Carefully select the appropriate categories for your book (after doing your research regarding the competitiveness and demand level for those categories).

73 – Write a compelling, benefit-driven book description to demonstrate the massive value readers will receive by reading your book.

74 – Verify your publishing territories, set your price, preview your book, and click "publish."

PROMOTE YOUR BOOK

75 – Start strong! In my experience, books that are promoted and marketed well in the first month of publication receive extra "love" and are promoted more during subsequent months by Amazon.

76 – Send out an email to your subscribers letting them know about your new book.

77 – Share news about your book on your Facebook, Twitter, and LinkedIn pages and ask your friends and fans to do the same.

78 – Remind reviewers to post reviews because the more positive reviews you have, the more likely people are to buy your book.

79 – If you've enrolled in Amazon's exclusive KDP Select program, select some free promotion dates so that you can give your book away for free.

80 – Notify the sites that promote free eBooks about your upcoming promo so that your book receives more exposure.

81 – Hire freelancers on Fiverr to write and/or submit press releases about your book.

82 – Use the KDP free promos and countdown deals to keep breathing new life into your book sales.

WRITE, PUBLISH, PROMOTE, REPEAT

Whoa!

Who said self-publishing was easy?

It is simple, but it is definitely not easy! It requires you to take full accountability for each step of the process (from writing to publishing to marketing). This means that you have to accept full responsibility for the success or failure of your book.

However, the great news is that there are hundreds of thousands of writers who are making a great living from eBook publishing – and you can too! I, for one, have found tremendous success as an ebook publisher, and this book details all the tools, tips, and techniques I use to keep my books in the Top 10 bestseller charts.

So, now that you're done publishing your book, what next?

The good news is – this book may be over, but your work isn't. **It's time to write and publish your next book!** The best form of marketing for an author is to write more books. The more books you write, the more fans you amass and the more books you sell.

Whether your aim is to make $2,000 or $20,000 per month from eBook sales, the formula is simple: **Write, publish, promote, repeat!**

Good luck!

To your success,

Akash Karia
www.AkashKaria.com

QUESTIONS OR COMMENTS?

I'd love to hear your thoughts.

Email me at: akash.speaker@gmail.com

IN HAVING ME SPEAK AT YOUR NEXT EVENT?

I deliver high-impact keynotes and workshops on productivity, time-management, success psychology and effective communication. Check out the full list of my training programs on *www.AkashKaria.com/Keynotes* and reach me on akash.speaker@gmail.com to discuss how we can work together.

GRAB $297 WORTH OF FREE RESOURCES

Want to learn the small but powerful hacks to make you insanely productive? Want to discover the scientifically proven techniques to ignite your influence? Interested in mastering the art of public speaking and charisma? Then head over to *www.AkashKaria.com* to grab your free "10X Success Toolkit" (free MP3s, eBooks and videos designed to unleash your excellence).

Be sure to sign up for the newsletter and join over 11,800 of your peers to receive free, exclusive content that I don't share on my blog.

IF YOU ENJOYED THIS

If you enjoyed this book, then check out Akash's other books:

HOW TO EFFORTLESSLY WRITE 1000+ WORDS - PER HOUR: THE 1K+ WRITING SYSTEM FOR WRITING NONFICTION BOOKS FASTER!
Do you find yourself struggling to write?

Do you wish you could write nonfiction books more quickly?

Is writing a slow and painful process for you?

In this book, bestselling author Akash Karia shares with you the exact techniques he used to go from writing 100 words per day to crunching out over 1500 words – per hour! These are the same techniques that allowed him to publish more than a dozen highly acclaimed #1 Amazon bestsellers over the span of a year.

Get the book here:
www.AkashKaria.com/WritingSystem

ANTI-PROCRASTINATION FOR WRITERS

Based on the international bestseller, "Ready, Set – Procrastinate" by Akash Karia, now EXPANDED AND UPDATED exclusively for writers.

"It truly is the best time in history to be a writer. The are no longer any boundaries. You can work with whomever you want to, at your own speed, get paid monthly, write about anything you want, do very little marketing, and still reach readers."
~ J.A.Konrath

In this book, Akash Karia shows you how to avoid procrastination and create a daily writing ritual. He reveals the same tools he used to write fourteen #1 internationally bestselling books in one year, while still maintaining his day-job as the chief commercial officer of a multimillion-dollar company.

Yes, these tools even work for people who are extremely busy, have families and have full-time jobs. These tools are simple techniques that are backed by hundreds of hours of intensive scientific research as well as Akash's experiences as a writer.

If you're ready to stop procrastinating, start writing and create a daily writing ritual, then get the book here: www.AkashKaria.com/WriterProcrastination

HOW SUCCESSFUL PEOPLE THINK DIFFERENTLY

"This book is packed with really wonderful mind sets, reframes, and psychology tips, all backed with references and real science. This is like the "best of the best" self help tips. A quick read, but a thanksgiving feast of food for thought."
~ Tim Brennan, #1 Bestselling Author of '1001 Chess Tactics'

Get the book here:
www.AkashKaria.com/SuccessBook

THE FINE ART OF SMALL TALK

"Akash Karia is a communications expert. He has the people skills to go with it. This book is easy to read and packed full of tips and techniques that you can implement immediately.

This isn't just about talking. He covers non-verbal cues, questioning and listening techniques as well as how to improve your charisma. He then steps it up a notch and tells you how leverage these techniques and take it to the next level.

It doesn't matter is you're an introvert or an extrovert, a confident talker or not, this book will have take aways for everyone."

~ Alastair Macartney, BASE Jumping World Champion & Bestselling Author of *Perfect Madness*

Get the book here:
www.AkashKaria.com/SmallTalk

HOW TO DELIVER A GREAT TED TALK: PRESENTATION SECRETS OF THE WORLD'S BEST SPEAKERS

"Akash has captured the best ideas, tools, and processes used by some of the best speakers and presenters in the world. He has distilled them in to a step-by-step, easy-to-read guide that will help you discover, develop, and deliver presentations which help you stand out from the crowd…Whether you are a new speaker learning the art of speaking, or a veteran looking for a new perspective, How to Deliver a Great TED Talk is a wise investment that can help take your speaking to a higher level."
~ Michael Davis, Certified World Class Speaking Coach

Get the book here:
www.AkashKaria.com/TEDTalkBook

ABOUT THE AUTHOR

Akash Karia is an internationally bestselling author who has twice been ranked the #1 Most Popular *Business & Money* author on Amazon. He earns a healthy passive income through his book sales, selling 100+ Kindle books per day. Akash is passionate about helping other people share their message and make passive income through their books. He has two other books in this series titled 'How to Effortlessly Write 1000+ Words – Per HOUR" and "Anti-Procrastination for Writers".

Akash currently lives in Tanzania where he works as the Chief Commercial Officer of a multi-million dollar company. When he is not writing or relaxing on a beach with a good book in his hands, he travels the world giving workshops and seminars. He is regularly sought-out by governments as well as businesses for his expertise on communication, motivation and peak performance psychology. You can inquire about Akash's availability through his website: **www.AkashKaria.com**

"Akash is THE best coach I've ever had!"
Eric Laughton, *Certified John Maxwell Trainer, United States*

Voted as one of the "10 online entrepreneurs you need to know in 2015"
The Expressive Leader

Featured as one of the "top 9 [online] presentations of 2014"
AuthorStream.com

"Akash is a phenomenal coach! The information I gained in just a few short hours is priceless."
Fatema Dewji, *Director of Marketing for billion-dollar conglomerate, MeTL, Tanzania*

"I loved the two days with Akash, which were filled with useful information. His passion and enthusiasm made the classes fun and exciting."
Pricilla Alberd, *Australia*

"The two days in Akash's workshop have been excellent, very informative and packed with knowledge...tons of practical, ready to use techniques."
Edyte Peszlo, *Sales and Procurement Manager, Thailand*

"I found the course content very relatable and explained in a way that way not only very easy to understand but also incredibly interesting."
Hayley Mikkos-Martin, *Australia*

"A rare talent who has much in store for you as an individual, and better yet, your organization."
Sherilyn Pang, *Business Reporter, Capital TV, Malaysia*

CONNECT WITH AKASH

Get your Free Anti-Procrastination Toolkit on:
www.AkashKaria.com

Check out more great books:
www.bit.ly/AkashKaria

Email for speaking-related inquires:
akash@akashkaria.com / akash.speaker@gmail.com

Connect on LinkedIn:
www.LinkedIn.com/In/AkashKaria

Printed in Great Britain
by Amazon